Best wishes from
Laos!

Matt J. Menger
O.M.I.

Vientiane, Laos

IN THE
VALLEY
OF THE
MEKONG

DEDICATED TO

The people of Laos, who have made my thirteen years as a missionary the happiest years of my life.

IN THE
VALLEY
OF THE
MEKONG

AN AMERICAN IN LAOS

MATT J. MENGER, O. M. I.

Foreword by H. Ross Perot

St. Anthony Guild Press, Paterson, N. J.

COVER DESIGN

The three-headed elephant is the official symbol of Laos. On the Lao national flag are the conjoined heads and fore-quarters of three white elephants standing on a platform under a tiered white parasol of state. This national symbolism has been inherited from the fourteenth-century kingdom of Lan Xang. The full traditional name of the country — Muong Lan Xang Hom Khao (Land of the Million Elephants and the White Parasol) — is emphasized in the flag and the state emblem.

In the present cover design a modern adaptation using the lotus blossom has been used as a framework.

Foreword

To truly appreciate *In the Valley of the Mekong,* the reader should have an opportunity to witness firsthand the people and the problems of that part of Southeast Asia.

The average citizen of the United States cannot imagine the poverty and need in Laos. Laos is half a world away from the United States. Much of the population of Laos is concerned solely with survival. The areas in our country that we consider as ghettos or slums would be upper middle-class neighborhoods in Laos. There is no area of the United States where living conditions of the poor can be compared to the life of the typical Laotian. Hunger, disease, poverty, a high infant-mortality rate, limited educational opportunities, and North Vietnam's continued ravaging of the countryside and the people plague this land.

Father Matt Menger has committed his life, and risks his life daily to help the people of Laos. He is a magnificent example, to all of us, of a man of God and a concerned American, who translated his concern into action, and his actions into orphanages, medical clinics, educational programs, agricultural developments, and religious training. He is probably the most beloved American in Laos. It was my good fortune to meet Father Menger and spend Christmas with him in Laos in 1969.

Father Menger is deeply involved in caring for the spiritual and physical needs of the people. I was particularly impressed with his ability to manage the small financial resources available to his effort in helping the people of Laos. Every citizen in this country can take deep pride in the work of Father Matt Menger. He is a living example of an outstanding man of God and, a United States citizen, to every Laotian that he meets and deals with.

This book, because it tells so much about Father Menger's activities and the people in Laos, will be a source of inspiration to young men and women who want to improve the world we live in. Father Menger is action-oriented. He is solution-oriented. The future of our nation and the world lies in the cumulative efforts of men of action like Father Menger — men dedicated to solving the problems that face us.

In a world made quite small by instant communications and air transportation, the need for people around the world to understand one another, to respect cultural differences, and to learn to work and live together in harmony becomes more and more essential to all of us. Father Menger and other dedicated Americans like him are truly making a better world for all of us, through their efforts.

My thoughts, prayers, and support go with this man of action — this man of God.

ROSS PEROT

Contents

VIII . . . . CONTENTS

IN THE
VALLEY
OF THE
MEKONG

THE ROYAL KINGDOM OF LAOS

CHAPTER ONE

The First Beginning

IT WAS A FEW MINUTES past midnight, November 21, 1956, when my DC-4 touched down on the soil of Indochina for the first time. Tan Son Nhut airport, Saigon!

I was en route to Laos and my new apostolate as a missionary in the Kingdom of the Million Elephants. I had arranged my ticket for a brief stopover in the "Paris of the Orient" — Saigon.

Hailing a battered taxi, I drove to town and checked in at the Continental Hotel. The lobby was deserted except for one elderly Vietnamese dozing in a chaise longue. Shaking him awake I asked, in French, for a room. As I was filling in the registration card, the lobby was suddenly engulfed in total darkness. All the lights blew out — all four of them! — plus the dingy little street lamp.

The wizened old man felt along the counter with his fingertips, searching for a match. As he struck a flame, the kerosene lamp threw eerie shadows on the wall. With a big smile, he explained, *"Panne d'électricité.* We have them often."

Picking up my bags, I followed the shadow of the man in the flicker of the lamp. Padding down the murky corridor, we turned, climbed the stairs, and reached my room on the second floor. As he turned the lock with his heavy

3

brass key, the door swung open. The room was big, the ceilings high and, I soon learned, the bed short. Very short!

At that time the Continental was THE hotel of Saigon. Conrad Hilton had nothing to worry about! The washroom at the end of the corridor offered a squat-type Asian toilet, and a variety of bugs which skittered across the dirty floor. A gasoline drum and a dipping pot furnished the necessary instruments for a shower — cold, that is.

Back in my room, I undressed and tiredly stumbled into bed. The thin mattress, plus the mosquitoes which attacked in squadrons, guaranteed insomnia. That night I learned the origin, and feeling, of the expression "Room and Board!"

Dawn finally crept over the horizon with an equally reluctant sun. Pulling my aching legs and back out of bed, I dressed hurriedly and walked over to the Cathedral. Saying my Mass in that century-old Gothic masterpiece, I breathed a special prayer of gratitude to Almighty God. I was in Asia, a missionary — at last!

Mass and meditation finished, I asked directions to 91 Duong Pasteur, the office of Catholic Relief Services (CRS). Monsignor Joe Harnett, the director of CRS, was absent on a field trip. But all the American staff was on hand: Chet Di Mauro, Lee Sanborn, Frank Broderick, and others. Their typical Yankee hospitality did much to still the butterflies in my stomach as I adjusted to the new world of Indochina.

"How can I see ALL of Vietnam in a couple of days?"

"You're lucky!" Chet answered. "We have six trucks loaded with CRS foods destined for the refugee camps along the road up to Hue. The convoy will leave tomorrow and stop at each camp to drop off food. You'll be able to see all of Vietnam right up to the seventeenth parallel. The area is not too safe, but...."

With a big grin he reassured me, "Don't look so scared. You'll have a Vietnamese army convoy all the way!"

Loaded with rice and powdered milk, the trucks of the convoy chugged out of Saigon. I was in the front seat of the second truck; the first carried our armed guard of Vietnamese soldiers.

Driving through Bien Hoa, we turned right onto Highway One. That night we slept at Xuan Loc. We didn't cover many miles that first day because we had stopped at a refugee camp to unload a couple of tons of supplies.

The second day our convoy reached Phon Thiet, a quiet little port town on the South China Sea. Following the coastline, we stopped at various refugee camps along the route.

Six a. m., the fifth day out of Saigon. In the village of Hoi An, I went to the small parish church to say Mass. As I introduced myself to the old Vietnamese pastor, his eyes lit up.

Speaking rapidly in French, he said, "Ah, Père Menger! I received a telegram for you yesterday. Since I did not know who you were, I returned it to the sender."

"What did it say?"

"I'm not sure," he replied. "You see, it was in English, and I know very little English."

Turning to Chet, I asked, "How fast can I get to Saigon?"

Seeing the concern on my face, the little priest interjected, "Ah, *mon père,* we have one plane a week that flies low over a cleared area."

Turning in the direction of his finger as he gestured toward a cluster of straggly huts, I heard: "If one wants to go to Saigon, he must signal the plane from that runway. You are very fortunate, *mon père*, for Sunday is the day the plane flies low." He smiled triumphantly as he concluded, "And today is Sunday!"

After I had said my Mass and eaten a light breakfast in the rectory, the pastor gave me a large serving of rice wrapped in a banana leaf. Chet handed me a can of sardines. Bidding farewell to Chet and my army convoy, I picked up my valise, rice, and sardines, and walked to the airstrip.

There was a lone tree on the side of the runway. I sat down and began to wait, and listen.

Nine a. m. Closing my breviary, I listened. Still no plane.

Noon came, the sun was directly overhead, and it was getting very hot. Opening the can of sardines and nibbling the rice, I realized I had no water. To walk the one mile back to town would mean to risk missing the plane.

Four o'clock. A faint hum in the distance. Louder. Yes, that was it! I jumped to my feet and ran out on the runway, waving my arms to catch the pilot's attention. The plane, a single-engine Beaver, buzzed the airstrip on its first pass. Seeing a passenger, the veteran French jungle pilot swung the vibrating Beaver around and landed.

The pilot did not cut the motors. I grabbed my valise, hopped aboard, swung down the heavy latch on the door, and gave him the thumbs-up "all-clear" signal. The Beaver shuddered like a man with convulsions. As the pilot pulled the stick forward, the docile little plane lunged ahead, down the bumpy strip, and up. Stashing my gear against the door, I looked around as I sat down. There were already six passengers aboard: one middle-aged Vietnamese man, one pig, and four ducks.

It was dark when we landed at Tan Son Nhut airport. I hurried over to Lee Sanborn's apartment in Saigon to see if he had the mysterious telegram. Letting me into his apartment, Lee silently handed me three telegrams. One was from the Oblate provincial in Texas; another from the Superior General in Rome; and one from Congressman Paul Kilday of Texas. All three telegrams said essentially the same thing: "Mother, brother killed automobile accident Mexico City, November 21. Return Texas immediately."

"O God, no!" The full impact of the message hit me. It couldn't be possible! Why, I had just said good-bye to them in San Antonio!

We had always been a close-knit family. Fleeting pieces of memories passed swiftly through my mind: Hank and I hunting on the farm; Mother laughing and teasing Dad; all of us attending Mass together each morning. . . . Now Dad was alone. "What must he be going through!" I wondered.

"What are you going to do, Father?" Lee asked quietly. I looked at him wordlessly. What could I do? I knew the tragedy would be a heavy cross for Dad. But still, what could I do if I went home? The accident had occurred more than a week before; undoubtedly the funeral was held as I was traveling up to Hue.

"I'm going on to Laos, Lee. I'll ask my new superior, Bishop Loosdregt, what he thinks I should do." Stuffing the three telegrams into my shirt pocket, I picked up my bags.

Early the next morning, I returned to Tan Son Nhut airport and boarded an Air Vietnam C-47 destined for Vientiane, Laos. The five-hour trip would be a slow one, with stops in Pakse and Seno.

As the plane soared into the sky and turned on its course for Vientiane, I leaned back in my seat. What would happen to my assignment to Laos? Would it be changed? Would I be sent back to Texas, or Rome?

Reaching into a small bag under my seat, I pulled out the notes I had made back in the Generalate in Rome. There was not too much information available on Laos. The few pages I had written were gathered from dusty archives and the atlas.

The newly independent Kingdom of Laos had been carved out of the Indochina States. Bordering on Communist China, Communist North Vietnam, Burma, Thailand, Cambodia, and South Vietnam, the tiny kingdom of ninety thousand square miles nestled in the midst of the former Indochina peninsula.

The history of Laos was a legendary one, passed on from generation to generation through the centuries. As legend has it, a man known as Khoun Borom was sent by the god of heaven to settle in the plain of Dien Bien Phu, with his two wives. A vine grew in their garden and on it were two great pumpkins. Khoun Borom took a red-hot iron and pierced the two pumpkins. Out came all the peoples of Laos, water buffalos, cattle, horses, and other animals, as well as gold and silver.

The legend continues to describe the pumpkin vine as achieving tremendous growth and thus casting an enormous shadow which spread over much of the country. It cut off the sun from the other crops. For a long time, the people said nothing because the vine furnished them with a means for traveling back and forth to heaven. However, eventually a brave man and his wife decided to chop down the enormous pumpkin. In the act they were crushed to death. The people rejoiced, however, for the sunlight was restored to the darkened country.

Khoun Borom's seven sons were sent to seven regions of the country: Luang Prabang, Xieng Khouang, Chiengmai, South Yunnan, North Fouhin, Ayutthaya, and Pegon. Thus began the Kingdom of Seven Sons, a history preserved in legend and unrecorded.

In 1353, Phi Fa, the crown prince of Luang Prabang, was driven from the kingdom in punishment for the seduction of one of the king's wives. Another version of his dismissal is that the crown prince had a son who was born with thirteen teeth. The king's soothsayers advised him to get this dangerous child out of the kingdom. So he was put on a raft and set adrift on the Mekong River, where a Buddhist priest found him and took him to the King of Cambodia in Angkor Wat.

The child, Fa Ngum, was raised in the court at Angkor and, when he was seventeen, was given one of the Cambodian princesses for his wife. When he was twenty-one years old, the King of Angkor gave him an army of ten thousand men and sent him back to conquer his grandfather's kingdom. He overcame the kings of Xieng Khouang, Luang Prabang, and Vientiane. The city of Vientiane originally was named Phay Nam, but its name was later changed to Vieng Kham, or "Walled City of Gold." Later still, the pronunciation was deformed to "Vieng Chan," which means "Walled City of Sandalwood." Today a similar pronunciation, "Vien Chan," is used for the city of Vientiane.

The Kingdom of Fa Ngum was called Lan Xang Hom Khao, "The Land of a Million Elephants and the White Parasol." It extended from the northern province, which bordered on China's Yunnan province, to Savannakhet in the south.

Dynastic disputes wracked the kingdom during the eighteenth century and resulted in the division of Lan Xang into weak principalities. During the late nineteenth century the French reunified the country and established its modern boundaries. The French ruled indirectly, allowing many traditionally prominent Lao families to maintain their social position. The Japanese occupied the country during World War II, and in 1945 declared the country to be independent. At the end of World War II the French granted Laos increasing self-government.

The Geneva Treaty of 1954 declared the Kingdom of Laos to be an independent and neutral nation and provided for the ultimate formation of a coalition government for Laos. The three separate factions which would make up this coalition government included the Royalists, led by Prince Souvanna Phouma, the Prime Minister. Loyal to the monarchy, the Royalists were strongly anti-Communist and tended to lean toward the West, rather than pursue a policy of total neutralism for Laos. The Neutralists were also anti-Communist but preferred that Laos follow a policy of total neutralism. Although they agreed with the Royalists on certain points, the Neutralists were inclined to be more tolerant of the Communists. The third faction was, of course, the Communists, led by Prince

Souphanouvong, half-brother of Prince Souvanna Phouma, the Prime Minister.

Despite the Geneva Treaty, conflicts among the three divergent groups led to a chaotic political situation in Laos. In 1957, the year after my arrival, Laos was experiencing the "lull before the storm." The storm broke out as civil war and led to the full-scale international war with the Communists which is still raging in Laos. The Geneva Treaty of 1954 guaranteed the establishment of a coalition government, which was actually set up in mid-1958. But by July of 1958 this government had collapsed. Since 1960 the Royalists and Neutralists have merged their forces into a single unified military force, and armed conflict has increased between them and the Communists.

The history of the Church in Laos is an equally stormy one. Rome was not built in a day, nor was the Catholic Church in Laos born in a day. It had taken 250 years of persecution and persistence.

The first attempt was made in 1642 by a young Jesuit stationed in Bangkok. After a brief sojourn in Vientiane and unsuccessful attempts at evangelization, Father Jean Marie de Leria returned to Siam.

He was followed twenty-nine years later by the Foreign Missionaries of Paris, who had been entrusted by Pope Alexander VII with the evangelization of thousands of square miles of unexplored mountains and jungles. As the years passed, more and more missionaries were sent to Laos. They came by pirogue up the Mekong River from Saigon and Phnom Penh. Others traveled by oxcart and horseback from Bangkok. Expeditions walked through the treacherous jungle mountains from Tonkin. But it was impossible to establish a beachhead.

As group after group of courageous young missionaries entered Laos, the number of martyrs increased. In 1878 fourteen priests arrived from Tonkin. By the end of that year, six had been murdered and seven had died from malaria and other tropical fevers. The sole survivor succeeded in escaping back to Tonkin, only to die a few months later because of broken health. The priests had been accompanied by sixty-two catechists. They, too, had been annihilated; forty-seven were murdered by bandits, fifteen died of malaria. Writing in his diary, one young missionary said, "At most, we can prepare the road for others." And prepare the road they did, although it was a bloody and painful one!

The Oblates of Mary Immaculate have the reputation of being "specialists in difficult missions." For this reason, Pope Pius XI assigned the entire northern half of Laos to the Oblates in 1934. At the time, there were less than a half-dozen priests in this vast area, equal in size to all of Italy.

The first Oblates, Fathers Jean-Henri Mazoyer, Étienne Loosdregt, and Jean-Paul Brouillette, arrived in Vientiane by boat, having traveled about 1250 miles from Saigon up the Mekong River. At that time there were no roads connecting Laos with Saigon. More missionaries arrived, but so did wars and persecutions: in 1938, Thailand invaded Laos; in 1941, the Japanese. Shortly after the Armistice of 1945, Communist infiltrators from North Vietnam began launching terrorist attacks throughout Laos. These attacks are continuing even at the present time.

* * *

Putting my notes back into my bag, I mused on my future as a missionary to Laos. Would my name be recorded in the roll of priests who had dedicated their lives to this pagan country? Or did destiny — and God — have other plans for me?

The C-47 banked, tilted its wings, and began its final approach into the small dirt landing strip of Vientiane's airport. As soon as the plane touched down and the passengers were cleared through Immigration, I flagged a taxi and drove to the American Embassy. There I met a former schoolmate of mine, Captain Bill Healey, who was now the assistant military attaché. Bill told me that Bishop Loosdregt, Vicar Apostolic of Vientiane, was in Paksane, one hundred miles down the Mekong. "I'll get a jeep, Father, and drive you to Paksane."

Gratefully I accepted Bill Healey's offer, glad for the few hours of companionship with my old friend. Next morning I set out with him for Paksane. As we jogged and bounced over and through the knee-deep wallows, the trip consumed an entire day. Dust clogged our throats, making conversation impossible. I was afraid to think too much about Dad's condition, or what the Bishop might tell me to do.

The monotonous journey behind us, we pulled into the driveway of the seminary in Paksane. Bishop Loosdregt, a veteran missionary and a calm, stately man, came out of the building and walked up to me.

Shaking my hand, he greeted me with a big smile. *"Bonjour, mon père.* Welcome to Laos!"

After returning his greeting, I pulled the crumpled telegrams out of my dusty shirt pocket, and handed them to the Bishop. "Ah, *mon Dieu!"* he said.

After I had explained the circumstances and my own feeling to the Bishop, we finally agreed to put the matter entirely in the hands of Rome. Twenty-four hours later a telegram was en route to our Generalate: "Menger prefers remain Laos. *Quid faciendum?*" Two days later a four-word response came from the Superior General. "Menger return Texas immediately."

Accepting the order from my superior, I packed my bag — and my dreams — and boarded a plane. Retracing my long journey, I passed through the same airports I had touched down at only days before. But now I was headed in the opposite direction. What the future — and God — held in store for me, I didn't know.

CHAPTER TWO

Three Words of Faith

As THE AIR LAOS PLANE LIFTED its nose off the concrete strip, I glanced at the "City of Sandalwood" as it slipped away under the wing. Leaning toward the window, I had a farewell glimpse of the muddy rice paddies of Vientiane which had greeted me only days before. "Who ever heard of a missionary with a three-day tour of duty?" I mused.

Gaining altitude, the pilot eased back on the throttle. The big plane cruised effortlessly through the blue sky and wispy clouds. As the plane sped forward, my mind turned backward.

How many times had Hank and I heard Mother say, "It's God's will!" For her, those three words ended all arguments, all protest. Mother had always had a deep and abiding faith in the goodness and mercy of God. Every childhood disappointment, every disaster or cross which came to our family was diminished by her confident trust in Almighty God. I needed that trust now. She and Hank were dead; Dad was alone in the big house; and my apostolate to Laos had been abruptly shelved. My well-ordered life had disintegrated. The only consolation was the memory of Mother saying, "It's God's will!"

We say "It's God's will" only when things don't go the way we want them to go. When the flight through life is smooth, we rarely give God a thought. It's much the same as flying through the atmosphere. Engrossed in the latest issue of *Time* or conversing with a fellow passenger, we don't give God a thought. But when the "Fasten seatbelts" sign flashes on and the 707 makes a couple of sudden drops, then our first thought is "Dear God." Forgotten and pushed out of our minds as we munch our way through the filet mignon and frozen peas, invariably he returns to our consciousness as lightning explodes in our path.

"Physician, heal thyself!" I thought ruefully. Is that why God was now tossing these huge black clouds in my path? The first twenty-seven years of my life had been an exceptionally smooth, cloudless flight.

* * *

It was on a cold evening in January, the twenty-fifth day, in the year of the depression, 1929. A newly born infant was placed in the room of cribs at the Santa Rosa Hospital in San Antonio. The tag on the infant's wrist was marked "Room 320." The hospital register showed the occupant of that room as "Mrs. Henry J. Menger, Sr." I was that child.

I should not have been born. At least that's what everyone said. God himself had hesitated many years. Through the early years of their marriage, my mother and father had hoped, and prayed, for a large family. The family doctor continued to shake his head, telling them: "Henry and Eleanor, it is just not possible. You can never have any children. You are hoping in vain." I'm sure he wanted to add, " . . . and you are praying in vain."

After my parents had hoped "in vain" for fifteen years and prayed in earnest, Hank was born. Baptized "Henry, Jr." he was the pride and joy of my parents, and a source of bafflement to our family doctor. The doctor called in several specialists for consultation. They, too, were baffled. But God wasn't — nor was my mother.

Then Eleanor and Henry Menger began more hoping, and more praying. This time the family doctor said: "All right, you had one miracle. But you can't have another. It is medically impossible." Again God hesitated. This time for three years. Then came that cold evening in January.

January 25 is the feast of the Conversion of St. Paul. The Epistle of the Mass for that day tells us how the fiery Saul had been struck from his horse. Looking up into the dazzling light, he cried, "Lord, what would you have me do?" On the anniversary of that miracle in the year 1929, the ten-pound second son of the Menger family lustily cried, "Here I am! Lord, what would you have *me* do?" Whether my mother and father continued their hoping and praying, I do not know. But I was their last child.

The morning after I was born, the Archbishop of San Antonio, Arthur Drossaerts, sent a note to Room 320. Of all the expensive cards and congratulatory letters Mother received, this one was the shortest, and made her the proudest. It was only three terse sentences. "God kept his promise. So will I! Let's make it three o'clock." Our Lord had indeed kept his promise to answer the prayer of whoever asks the Father anything in his name. The Archbishop would keep *his* promise to baptize the child my parents had prayed for.

That afternoon the Archbishop of San Antonio, in a plain black cassock, surrounded by a dozen Santa Rosa Sisters in their white hospital garb, leaned over me and said, "William Francis Mathias, *ego te baptizo....*" Less than twenty-four hours old, I ceased being a pagan and was enrolled in the litany of Christians.

At the time of my birth, my parents were living in the old Menger homestead on Blum Street. That one story, hand-hewn stone dwelling had become quite a landmark in San Antonio. My great-grandfather had arrived in Texas, emigrating from Germany, back in the 1840's. There weren't many homes in San Antonio then, so he fenced in a fairly large chunk of pasture land facing on the town square, which was known as "Alamo Plaza." The land was adjacent to the Franciscan church which had become famous as The Alamo.

When he married, my great-grandfather built a large, southern-style frame home having several extra bedrooms. When the ranchers from outlying spreads would come to town, old Will Menger would invite them over to spend the night. Soon those extra bedrooms became San Antonio's guest house. As the number of people coming to town kept increasing, Great Grandpa added more bedrooms and enlarged the dining room. One day he painted a large sign and hung it from the second-floor balcony. "The Menger Hotel." Quickly word spread through all of south Texas: "San Antonio has a hotel!"

One day Great-Grandpa Menger wrote to an old brewmaster friend in Germany, inviting him to come to San Antonio. The following year, Mr. Degan arrived. Setting to work, he and Will Menger enlarged the basement and installed the enormous German stills. Soon the famous lager was dripping from the stills, and the sign in front was repainted to read, "Menger Hotel and Degan Brewery."

The hot, dry climate of south Texas left San Antonians with an unquenchable thirst. Kegs of Menger-Degan brew poured down the throats of cowboys, ranchers, and businessmen. But the Yankee guests from the north were more sophisticated. They wanted their beer cold. My great-grandfather wrote another letter, this time to a friend in Boston, ordering a regular supply of ice to be shipped to his hotel. The ice would be sent by boat to the nearest port, a little town on the Gulf of Mexico, not far from the mouth of Lavaca Bay. To ensure that the ice would arrive as quickly as possible over the hot Texas plains, my great-grandfather set up his own stagecoach service.

One day the desk clerk at the Menger Hotel registered a newly arrived group of visitors from Washington, D. C. They were American soldiers with official orders to "establish a military garrison along the U. S. southern border to protect the United States from attacks by Mexico." When the small band of American soldiers tied their horses to the hitching post in front of the hotel, they decided this was far enough south. That evening in the dining room, they told my great-grandfather of their mission. Their orders had also included the instructions that "The land for the new garrison must be donated. The U. S. Army does not have money for such purchases." I don't know if Will Menger was fired by patriotism or his flare for business; nevertheless, the next day he deeded to the U. S. Army a fair-sized corner of his pasture. San Antonio thus acquired Fort Sam Houston!

When I came on the scene in 1929, our neighbors were getting too close. Joske's of Texas, J. C. Penney's, the

Woolworth store, the Federal Building and Post Office had completely surrounded our home. So my parents rented our house next to the Menger Hotel and moved to the Menger farm a couple of miles outside the city limits. Dad continued to drive to his office in town each morning, working as the publisher of the *Southern Messenger,* the first and only Catholic newspaper in Texas. The paper had been founded by my grandfather, and Dad was carrying on the tradition.

The early years of my life were very happy. I soon learned to speak, and I enjoyed every word. One evening at supper, Mother looked at Hank and me and gave us some advice. I'll never forget it. What she told us that evening has helped me tremendously through the years which have followed.

In her gentle but firm voice she said, "For every language you learn, you are another man." During that meal, Mother and Dad began making of each of their sons "another man" — in German! From that supper on, whenever I wanted anything, be it a bicycle or a hamburger, I had to learn the German words, or do without! I soon learned all the important words, and many others, too! Thus, my maternal language became German.

When I was five, Mother took me to the Ursuline Academy in downtown San Antonio and enrolled me in the first grade on the day school began. Not very long afterward, I was back home.

"Matt, why are you home?"

"Sister told me to go," I mumbled.

"I know that, but WHY did she tell you to go home?" Mother insisted. "If you don't tell me, I'll ask Sister myself!"

"It wasn't my fault, Mom. She asked me a couple of questions but they didn't make sense. There's something wrong with her. She doesn't speak my language!"

"Mine," of course, was German; "hers" was English. Told by Sister not to come back until I had learned "hers," I spent the next few months at home, studying English!

When I did return to Ursuline Academy, I was met by my classmates and promptly nicknamed "Sauerkraut," which they soon shortened to just plain "Kraut."

The following year Ursuline Academy was converted into a girls' school only, and Hank and I transferred to St. Martin's Hall, which was directed by the Sisters of Divine Providence. Because two of my father's sisters were Divine Providence nuns, we became, and remained, adopted "nephews."

"Busy" is the best adjective to describe those days of my childhood near San Antonio. Our nearest church was the Oblate Fathers' seminary two miles away, and their earliest Mass was 5:15 a. m. Sleet or sunshine, the Menger family, all four of us, attended that Mass each morning. Back home my brother and I would rush out to the barn to milk a couple of Jersey cows. Dad would then drive us eight miles to St. Martin's. Home at five p. m., we again milked the Jerseys, did our homework, and tumbled into bed.

It never occurred to either Hank or me to complain. Life was wonderful! Our back yard was 110 acres of pasture land. Horses stood in the barn waiting for a wild gallop through the mesquite; goats and cows became our friends; and the nearby woods were filled with ideal hunting: deer, wild turkeys, and opossums. Unfortunately the farm also had many other less desirable creatures of God:

rattlesnakes, tarantulas, and scorpions were lying in wait for our dusty bare feet.

On my eighth Christmas, Dad gave Hank and me a unique present: four small Jersey calves. We were in business! Calling ourselves "The Menger Brothers Cattle Company," my brother and I formed a corporation; he was the president, I was the treasurer. We never counted the hundreds of gallons of milk we lugged out of the barn, nor the hours of hard work spent grooming and caring for the cows. As the years went by, we decided to branch out. Using our profits from the cows, we bought two hundred Leghorn chickens. Following the chickens came one hundred turkeys, then a few ducks, and finally the goats. All of the responsibility for the menagerie was ours, and it was a rugged routine. But we didn't care. Counting the nickels, dimes and dollars we had in our bank account, we were within sight of our goal.

On December 24, 1940, as we were trimming the six-foot tree in the living room, a good friend of the family drove up. He was a car dealer in San Antonio and that day was driving a flashy, brand-new Chevrolet station wagon. After an exchange of Christmas greetings, Mom and Dad went out to admire their friend's new car. Hank and I noticed the envy in their eyes, for they had always wanted a station wagon. Dad even opened the door and tried out the driver's seat.

Hank winked at the visitor. Catching the signal, the visitor fumbled in his pocket and handed Dad an envelope. With Mom peering over his shoulder, he opened it. Inside was just an ordinary Christmas card with the following greeting carefully penned:

"To Mom and Dad,
the finest in the whole world.
Merry Christmas!

THE MENGER BROTHERS CATTLE COMPANY
Hank, President
Matt, Treasurer"

The visitor handed Dad the keys and smiled, "Henry, would you mind driving me home..., in your new station wagon?"

* * *

"Why did you become a priest, Father?" How many times I had been asked that question! My answer used to be, "Because I loved God." That response was so simple that I always wondered why people asked such a simple question. As the years rolled by, I realized that my answer really wasn't exact. It should have been reversed to "Because God loved me."

On September 8, 1941, I entered St. Anthony's, the Oblate Fathers' minor seminary in San Antonio. Hank had preceded me into the seminary by three years. As small boys on the farm, we had made a pact: Hank and Matt were to be the twentieth century's Peter and Paul.

My five years at St. Anthony's passed quickly and happily. So did the following year at the novitiate, the "boot camp" of religious life. I pronounced my first vows as an Oblate of Mary Immaculate on May 31, 1947. In September I was to commence my seven years of philosophy and theology at the Oblate major seminary just two miles

from home. At least, that's what I thought. God — and
Rome! — thought otherwise. Fall came and I began my
philosophy and theology, but it was in a seminary six thousand miles from home, in Rome.

Life wasn't plush at 5 Via Vittorino da Feltre, the
Oblate seminary. Far from it. There was no central, or
any other, heating during the cold Italian winters. Our
dorms were on the third floor. To take a shower, one had
to walk a long corridor, down three flights of stairs, into
the basement. Before going to bed at night, each seminarian would carry his basin down to the showers, fill it
with water, then up the three flights of stairs so that he
could shave in the morning. During the winter months,
we would have to crack through the film of ice to get
to the water.

In 1947 Italy was staggering through the postwar days.
Food was scarce and expensive. For three years we had
no butter. The first six months in Rome I never saw a
piece of bread. After that period, when things got better,
each seminarian would get fifty grams (the equivalent of
two slices) of bread a day. For breakfast we would have
one cold potato, washed down with a murky, black brew
which substituted for coffee. Sugar was a rarity. The seminarians took it all in stride, while the Fathers struggled
with the problems of feeding a pack of growing boys on
the few ration coupons they were allotted.

I often recalled Mom's statement that for every lan-
guage one becomes another man — indeed my years in
Rome were centered around this fact. Having mastered
German, English, and Spanish in Texas, I set to studying
Latin and Greek. In the Oblate house our official languages
were French and Italian, of which I knew nary a syllable.

THREE WORDS OF FAITH 25

Our classes and exams at the Gregorian University were in Latin, and a fluent knowledge of Greek and Hebrew was also required for our supplementary reading assignments. Plowing through the philosophers Gredt and Descartes, I worked my way up to theology and became friends with Bellarmine and Aquinas.

But Rome was more than cold spuds for breakfast and hard Greek in class. Rome was the major basilicas and tiny churches tucked away in unexpected piazzas. With Père Drouart, the seminary superior, we would spend days exploring the catacombs. The Scala Sancta and the Sistine Chapel, the Coliseum, the pompous canonizations in St. Peter's and the quiet Masses in the Mamertine Prison became part of my everyday life. I was in the empire of the Romans, the heart of Christianity, and every day was exciting and happy. I gained the reputation of a walker, wandering through the Italian countryside and exploring the narrow side streets of Rome.

Seven years sped by, culminating in the most unforgettable day of my life: ordination in the Basilica of St. John Lateran on April 18, 1954. Seminary days were ended. My class, the men with whom I had eaten, studied, and prayed for the past years, began to receive their assignments. Bidding them farewell as they left for Basutoland, Haiti, Cotabato, Shikoku, I waited. Finally the Superior General read out, "Père Menger...." There was a short pause. The Superior General, Very Reverend Leo Deschatelets, continued, "...you are hereby assigned to the Generalate in Rome."

The next twenty-four months I spent digging through dusty manuscripts in the Postulation Office of the Oblate Generalate. I was doing research on the causes of canonization for six Oblates, including our founder, Bishop Charles Joseph DeMazenod.

It began to appear that God had his own plans for the twentieth century's would-be Peter and Paul. After his ordination, Hank had been assigned as a professor in the Oblate seminary in Mexico City. And here I was in Rome, manning a desk and a file cabinet as I worked on the causes of canonization. Both of us were a long way from the primitive mission fields we had envisioned for ourselves when we made that pact so many years before.

My world evolved into a pleasant routine of interesting work, and living in Rome. All of this came to an end one evening when the Superior General told me I was to be assigned to Laos. The Geneva Treaty of July, 1954, had dissolved the Indochina States, and Laos was to receive complete independence. Word filtering through official circles was that ALL French citizens would have to leave Laos.

Walking in the garden of the General House, Father Deschatelets said: "Bishop Loosdregt has asked me to send him an English-speaking priest. We need a man who can live in a French-speaking religious community, adjust himself to life in an Oriental culture, and bridge the gap with the international community."

I knew that all of our missionaries in Laos, except two, were French citizens. Furthermore, the United States, England, Australia, and other English-speaking countries were initiating diplomatic relations with Laos.

With a twinkle in his eye, Father Deschatelets said: "So, Father, the Council decided. You're it!" His voice fading away to a whisper, he said: "It's a difficult mission, a dangerous assignment. God bless you, my son."

A few weeks later, I boarded a plane at Ciampino air terminal in Rome. With permission from my superiors to spend a few weeks in Texas saying good-bye to my family, I packed my books and gear and arranged my itinerary. Rome, New York, San Antonio, a few days to be spent visiting Saigon, and then Vientiane, and my new apostolate as a missionary to Laos.

The few days in Texas passed swiftly. Keeping Mother busy sorting my clothes and packing, I kept both our minds off the inevitable day of parting.

Offering Mass at St. Gregory's, I gave Mom and Dad Holy Communion. A quiet breakfast, and we all piled into the car headed for the airport. Mom's courage sustained her up to the departure gate. Breaking into tears, she sobbed: "Please don't go! Please don't go!"

"Mom, I have to go. You know you wanted both Hank and me to be missionaries. You and Dad sacrificed to make it possible for us to be priests. Now we have to keep our end of the bargain."

"But it's so dangerous over there. That awful food.... Anything could happen!"

Putting my arms around her, I said, "Mom, always remember — when my number is up, God will take me, no matter where I am."

Stifling her tears, crumpling her handkerchief into a knot, she whispered, "I know, son."

Kissing me good-bye, Dad's arm around her shoulders, she turned away as I walked through the gate and boarded the plane.

A couple of weeks later, both Mom and Hank were dead. And I was aboard a plane carrying me back to San Antonio!

CHAPTER THREE

A Promise Kept

"FASTEN YOUR SEATBELT, Father. We're coming in to San Antonio. The stewardess jolted me out of my reverie. "I'll bet you're glad to get home, aren't you?" With a cheery smile, she continued down the aisle.

"If she only knew!" I thought. Only a few weeks before, I had stepped into this same terminal. That afternoon I had been met by Dad, Mother, and Hank. Smiles, hugs, and laughter marked my return to Texas after nine years in Rome.

This afternoon only Dad was at the fence. There was a smile on his face, but it was the smile of a patient after the doctor had amputated a limb of his body. Behind the faint smile was a tired, and tried, countenance.

On the drive in from the airport, Dad gave me all the details. "Just after you left for Laos, Hank telephoned," Dad said. My brother, Father Henry Menger, had been teaching in the Oblates' minor seminary in Mexico City. Dad went on: "Hank asked Mother to fly to Mexico and spend a few weeks with him."

As Dad spoke, I could see what Hank had in mind. He realized that Mother would take my departure for Laos very hard. The family knew that we were normally assigned to foreign missions for life, and that our vacations at home averaged once every ten years. A few weeks of sightseeing and fun in Mexico would help Mother over the hump. It was typical of Hank, always thinking of the other person. A few days after his call, Mother flew to Mexico City.

The two weeks passed quickly, and she enjoyed every minute of it. The day before her return to San Antonio, Hank took Mother, and three other friends, to a fiesta at a bullfighters' ranch just outside Mexico City. On their return that evening, a truck with no headlights hit them head-on.

In the screech of broken glass and twisted metal, my mother was heard to mumble, "Jesus, Mary, Joseph!" She died instantly. Hank, although he had a mangled right arm and multiple internal injuries, pulled all four passengers from the crumpled station wagon. Stumbling into the highway, he flagged a passing car to take the three critically injured to a hospital. Despite the pleas of rescuers that he go with them, he urged the lone car to get to the hospital quickly with the other critical cases. He would wait. Sitting next to Mother's body, he administered the Last Sacraments to her, and waited on the highway forty-five minutes before another car arrived to carry them into the city. Hank died shortly after his arrival at the hospital. The other passengers all survived.

Dad, a quiet man, took the loss heroically. Fearing a heart attack, the doctor urged sedation and bed rest. Six a. m. each morning found Dad kneeling in the parish church near our home, attending Mass and receiving Communion, as he had every day of his life. His silent courage and strong faith held the remnants of our family together during those dark days.

I was home for ten months. Dad and I drifted into a semblance of normal life, and the days passed swiftly. We did not speak of Laos.

* * *

Santa Rosa Medical Center in San Antonio is one of the most famous medical facilities in the United States. Staffed by the Incarnate Word nuns, the hospital had long been a familiar part of my boyhood life. And, of course, I had been born there.

With time lying heavily on my hands, I arranged with the hospital directors for a "crash" course in medicine. In Rome I had had one year of medical training at the Knights of Malta med school for missionaries. But I knew that I could use all the medical skill I could cram into my brain when my "practice" began in Laos. God bless those saintly Sisters and dedicated doctors at Santa Rosa! They had the patience of saints in teaching me "all" the pre-med studies in six short months.

With my green scrub suit as mufti, I quickly immersed myself into the routine of wards and lab work. The young nurses, spotting my lack of a wedding ring, began inquiring who the new "intern" was. I was twenty-seven at the time, tall and blond! The hospital directors and I had judged that it would be best not to inform the patients, or nurses, that I was a priest. Thus, snooping to get the lowdown on "Doctor Menger," the nurses were always put off with an evasive answer. This only whetted their appetite! Their female instincts rose to the surface and they began the hot pursuit of their latest quarry.

Young and naïve, I accepted their helpful advice and friendliness, not realizing they were really flirting, and without seeing the dark glares of the staff doctors (all married) whose professional needs were being sadly neglected. One evening there was a program in the nurses' home. Many eyes opened, and many hearts sank, as "Intern" Menger walked in in his Roman collar!

Lab work was one of my first, and favorite, assignments. One morning I was asked to go to Room 420, take a blood sample, and pick up the morning urine specimen. Mission accomplished!

Padding down the hospital corridor, the urine bottle delicately covered with a towel and balanced on a tray, I turned the corner and stopped dead! Straight ahead was an old friend of my mother's — Paula Schurman. Elegant in a tailored suit and a mink stole, she was sauntering down the hall in my direction.

Although I had not seen her in many years and was dying to talk to her, I couldn't "blow my cover." Too many nurses and patients were around! Taking a deep breath, I marched ahead, gripping the urine pot and keeping my eyes forward. As I passed Paula, I noticed out of the corner of my eye that she stopped, turned around, and stared. Double-timing it down the hall, I turned the corner and ducked out of sight.

Later that week, Paula had dinner with Dad and me. As she came in the door of our house, she threw her arms around me for a quick hug. Then she said, "You know, Matt, I spotted an intern in Santa Rosa the other day who looked just like you. Isn't that strange! Did you know you had a double?"

During those six months at Santa Rosa, I kept a cassock hanging in the emergency room. Many times a week, I had to slip it on hurriedly over my scrub suit. It's strange how many people decide to go to confession or ask to be baptized when they are hauled into the emergency room and told that their condition is critical. Being an "intern-priest" can be very practical!

The work at Santa Rosa was immensely interesting. Dad seemed to be readjusting after the shock of the tragedy, and life was fairly normal again. Then one evening, the telephone rang.

"Matt, one of our missionaries in Tehuantepec, Mexico, is critically ill. We have to evacuate him immediately. Can you replace him?"

The caller was our provincial, Father Larry Seidel. Without waiting for my reply, he continued, "Be at the airport tomorrow morning at seven a. m. We've booked an Eastern Airlines flight for you to Mexico City. There you'll connect with a flight to Oaxaca. The superior of the Tehuantepec mission will meet you and jeep you the last 250 miles. Stay there until I send you further orders."

Mumbling a quick "O. K.!" I hung up the phone, and began throwing things into a bag. The takeoff, change of planes, and drive to Tehuantepec went smoothly. After a night at our central mission, we drove another fifty miles out through the mountains to a smaller mission. There I was introduced to my sacristan-cook, to my horse and jeep, and given a map of my parish. Thirty-two villages — two reachable by jeep, thirty by horseback — fifty thousand Catholics and myself, the only priest!

"We'll come to pick you up when Father Ed gets out of the hospital." With an *"adios"* and a wave, Father

Robert Biasiolli threw his faithful jeep into low gear. I stood for a few minutes watching the dust settle. The sun was just beginning to slip behind the towering mountains off in the distance.

Only months before, I had been a very contented priest, happy in my work as a secretary in Rome. Then a missionary to Laos, a pagan kingdom in Asia. And here I was, pastor to fifty thousand Tehuano Indians in southern Mexico! "Lord, I hope you know what you're doing!" I thought, as I turned and walked into my adobe rectory.

It was a very busy and happy life: baptizing the babies, treating the sick, anointing the dying. Weeks rolled by, eight of them. Then one day a jeep rolled in. Father Ed, a bit pale but game, was ready for the harness again. I packed my small bag, tossed it in the back of the jeep, and slowly wended my way down the dusty main — and only — street. Clumps of kids, men and women, all waved and shouted, *"Padrecito! Vaya con Dios! Vaya con Dios!"*

Upon my return to San Antonio, there were several letters waiting for me. One from Bishop Loosdregt in Vientiane, the other from Father Deschatelets in Rome. Both letters said essentially the same thing: "Stay in Texas as long as you deem necessary for your father's sake."

I was longing to get back to Laos, to begin my missionary apostolate. But how would Dad take it? That farewell would be very painful for both of us. It would be a good many years before I'd see Texas again. Would Dad still be living? Five or ten years can be a long time when a man is in his seventies. I decided to wait, and watch, a bit longer.

In Laos there are not only few doctors, but even fewer mechanics. So I decided to get some "on-the-job" training in automotive repair. A telephone call to Joe Wagner, owner of the Wagner Garage, and I was hired.

I reported for my new job — no longer in a green scrub suit, but now in blue coveralls. Adjusting ignition points, changing brake shoes, flushing fuel systems filled my days. One morning a well-known San Antonio surgeon brought his Buick in for a tune-up and other minor adjustments. The garage foreman promised him it would be ready by four o'clock.

At four p. m. sharp, the surgeon returned. His car wasn't quite finished. He immediately began telling the foreman what he thought about the garage. Striding angrily through the garage, looking for his car, he spotted it — and a pair of feet protruding from underneath. Grabbing one of them, he shook it violently, saying, "Hey, buddy! When the hell are you gonna finish?"

After he had released my foot, I rolled out from under his car. I've never seen a more baffled look. Despite my greasy face and coveralls, he recognized me as the "intern" who had accompanied him on several of his ward visits. (He didn't know "Intern" Menger was really "Father" Menger.)

Scratching his head, he muttered, "I'll be damned! An intern working as a mechanic! Garage business MUST be good!"

* * *

Coming home from the garage one evening, I scrubbed off the oil and grease, and slipped into clean clothes for dinner. After we had finished eating, we were sitting in the living room. Dad puffed on a cigar, rocking gently in his favorite old rocker. I could tell he was a bit more pensive than usual.

"Son," he began, "many years ago when you entered the seminary, your mother and I promised each other that we would never hinder your vocation in any way. It wasn't easy to give both you and Hank to God, but we made our promise. Now Mother is gone...." His voice trailed off.

I sat silently, expectantly. There seemed no way to make it easier for the poor old man. Tears welled up in his eyes. Taking another puff on his cigar, he continued: "Providence recalled you. But I feel that God still wants you to carry out a job for him in Laos. And I know Mother would want me to keep our promise."

Tears trickled down the crevices of his lined face, which had aged so much in the past few months. "Don't worry about me, son. I may not live to see you again. But after all, you and Mother and Hank and I will all be together in heaven one day." He tried to go on — but could not. He really did not have to.

On October 3, the feast of St. Thérèse of Lisieux, Patroness of the Missions, I offered my Mass in our parish church and gave Dad Holy Communion. After breakfast, he drove me to the airport. Soon I had tightened my safety belt and the plane was streaking down the runway. Glancing out the window, I could see hundreds of waving, laughing people. Searching the crowd, I found one tall, stately, elderly gentleman. He, too, was waving with his right hand, but in his left hand was a handkerchief. "There stands a REAL missionary — a real hero," I thought to myself, as I reached for my handkerchief.

CHAPTER FOUR

The Mekong Again

"LICE!" I yelled.

The chubby waiter, his gold tooth shimmering in the brightly lit dining car, wearily shook his head.

"No! No! Not flied lice. FLIED LICE!!!" he said emphatically. Tossing the greasy towel over his left arm, he heaved a deep sigh. His troubles with the *faleng* (foreigner) had started a few moments before, when I walked into the dining car in search of food.

Scouring the menu for something edible, I gave up, handing the menu back to the waiter. The unintelligible curls, dashes, circles and squiggles of the Thai script had no meaning. As a result of asking what he would recommend, we were now arguing over his astounding suggestion. Finally, the light dawned, and I recalled the Oriental habit of substituting "l's" for "r's"!

"Oh, fried rice!"

With a weak smile, he nodded his head and said, "Yah! Yah! Flied lice!"

The plane which I had boarded in San Antonio deposited me in Bangkok, the capital of Thailand. Twenty-four hours later, I was on a train destined for Nongkhai, on the border of Laos.

Munching my "flied lice," I glanced out the window of the dining car. The train was rickety, certainly not a

relative of the late beloved Twentieth Century Limited.
The road bed was filled with curves and bumps, so that
the passengers were jostled from side to side. After twelve
hours of hanging on, we lurched in our seats as the train
came to an abrupt halt. We had come to the end of the
railroad tracks!

Stepping out onto the platform, I approached a shab-
bily dressed Thai who was standing nearby. "How do I
get to Laos from here?"

"You can't. You have to wait until tomorrow."

Picking up my bags I set out for the nearest, and only,
Catholic church in town. As dusk settled over the village
of Udorn, I came to the decrepit plank fence which marked
the episcopal residence of Monsignor Clarence Duhart,
C. Ss. R., then Apostolic Prefect of northeastern Thailand.
The frame house was more aptly suited for an impoverished Thai family. Nevertheless, nothing could lessen the
warm and friendly hospitality of Monsignor (now Bishop)
Duhart.

The following day, I bought a ticket for the *loat me*
(mother truck) which served as the local bus between
Udorn and Nongkhai. The three-hour trip provided excitement and kept us on the alert, clinging to the seats
to avoid falling out. Chickens in bamboo baskets, tied to
the top of the ancient truck, screeched and screamed. Native women spit betel nut juice, heedless of the direction
of the wind. The driver hunched over the wheel, his foot
down to the floorboard, as he raced an invisible dragon
to the border of Thailand.

Nongkhai at last! And my first sight of the mighty
Mekong, the "Mother of Life." Formed in the Himalayas
of Tibet, the river flows southeast, passing through Yun-

nan province in southern China. Continuing on its 2,600-mile journey, the Mekong snakes its way through Indochina, forming vast and fertile deltas before it empties into the South China Sea.

I scooped up my dust-covered bags and clambered down the rutted path. Stepping gingerly into a narrow flat-bottomed pirogue, trying not to notice the water which lapped over the sides, I sat rigidly as the boatman swung the tiny craft into the mainstream of the powerful current.

As I disembarked on the other side of the Mekong, I set foot in Laos, for the second time! Climbing up the bank, skidding, dropping my bags, using tree stumps and roots for footholds, I worked my way to the top. While searching for the expected immigration office, I spotted a sentinel house painted in red and white stripes. The miniature guardhouse served as Immigration, Customs, and official processing station for all passengers entering into, and going out of, the Royal Kingdom of Laos.

Lugging my gear, I sauntered over to the house. The immigration official was on duty all right! He sat on a stool in the guardhouse, sound asleep! It was siesta time, the two-hour period after lunch, the most sacred hours of the Lao day.

I called several times. "Sir, ... er, ahem! Mister...." As his snores rose to ever-increasing crescendos, I gave up the futile struggle. Walking down the road, I headed for the lone taxi, which stood in the early afternoon sun.

I shook the driver awake and asked him to take me into Vientiane. Muttering something in Lao, no doubt referring to stupid *falengs* who arrived at siesta time, he scraped his gears and we were off.

Again I clung to the door frame as the driver chased the invisible dragon which had apparently crossed over from Thailand with me. Fifteen miles later, in a cloud of dust, a screech of brakes, and the smell of burning rubber, I made my entrance at *Le Sacré-Coeur.*

Le Sacré-Coeur, which served as cathedral for the Bishop, parish for the entire city, residence for priests and chancery office, stood sedately under the towering flame trees. Greeted by Père Fernand Chotard, I was led into the rectory and welcomed into the family. My life as a missionary in Laos had officially begun.

The next morning I went to pay a courtesy call on the American Ambassador, and to notify the embassy that they had another American citizen on their hands. My naïve mental picture of embassies had not prepared me for the sight of the dilapidated two-story wooden structure which served as diplomatic headquarters for the United States Government.

Climbing the rickety spiral staircase, I emerged onto a small landing. Ahead were two doors: one closed, one open. No one was in sight.

"Anybody here?" I called out as I walked through the open door. Silence. Continuing through the first room I poked my head through the half-open doorway of a small, inner room.

"What the hell are you doing?" The indignant, booming voice startled me to attention. "How did you get in here?"

Turning, I saw a tall, blustery American, his chin jutting out as he confronted this "menace" to the security of the American Embassy. Calmly I answered, "The door was open. I walked in."

Blushing a deep beet-red, he answered my inquiry as to directions to the Ambassador's office by pointing toward a closed door. As I walked out after my interview with the Ambassador, I noticed the hatchet on the wall, and the carbine and shotgun standing in the corner. When I reached the outer door, I came face to face with a boldly lettered sign: "KEEP LOCKED ALWAYS! SECURITY IS IMPORTANT!"

"Ah so!" I thought.

It was good to be back "home" at last. I spent the first few days in Vientiane, a sluggish, dusty city. It was hard to believe that the dirt paths, bamboo huts, and water buffalos ambling down the road were part of the capital of the latest independent nation in the world family.

The number of English-speaking residents had increased considerably. Fifteen Canadians were attached to the U. N. International Control Commission; four British had arrived to set up their new embassy; fifty-two Filipinos were working for the U. S. Operations Mission, United States Information Service (USIS), and the Operation Brotherhood Hospital. Almost four hundred Americans were in Vientiane, attached to the various U. S. government offices: Embassy, USOM, USIS, and three engineering-construction firms (Radar, Universal, and Pioneer). The overall population of Vientiane had soared to 35,000!

With Bishop Loosdregt's words ringing in my ears ("Go to the seminary in Paksane and study Lao"), I set off early one morning for the marketplace. Traveling had always interested me, and I looked forward to a leisurely bus trip to Paksane, one hundred miles down the Mekong.

As I worked my way through the teeming market, jostled by the noisy crowd and women shouldering pots of *khao phoun,* I spotted the Paksane bus. Shades of Greyhound! The bus was a relic of World War II days. A dilapidated army truck salvaged from the French, it had been "renovated" into the only public transportation system serving the Vientiane-Paksane communities.

The *loat me* (mother truck) sat in the shade of a flame tree. The rear bed sagged as it was loaded with men, women, and children. The flatbed had two wooden benches loosely bolted to the floor. There was no roof — and darn little to hang on to!

With the bus already overloaded with passengers, screaming babies, and snapping ducks, the driver was busily and loudly shouting instructions to the passengers to "move to the rear of the bus," so he could add several sacks of rice and two bicycle tires.

My six-foot-three-inch frame was folded between a young mother holding a diaperless baby and a bamboo cage of squawking hens. My legs encircled one of a dozen large earthenware crocks. I noticed that the crocks were leaking. As the branches of the flame tree stirred in the breeze, the fragrance from the crocks reached my nostrils. *Nam pa* — the fermented fish paste, a favorite Lao seasoning!

The courageous and overloaded "mother truck" set out down the dusty road. Eleven hours later we arrived in Paksane, as the sun was setting. Everyone was exhausted and ill-tempered. The bed of the truck was runny with *nam pa,* the babies cried hungrily, and I breathed a sigh of relief.

Paksane was one of the "big" cities of Laos. Its population: three thousand! With Père Jean Hanique as my teacher, I set to work studying the Lao language. Ten hours a day, seven days a week, my tongue twisted around the nasal syllables of this Oriental language.

There are several "musts" which just have to be learned. And the sooner they are learned, the less embarrassing — as I soon sadly experienced! The meaning of a word depends (1) on the length of the vowel — long or short; (2) on whether the consonant is aspirated — or not; (3) on which of the five tones you hit.

For example, take the three letters "K-A-O." "Kao" is a very common word and can mean any of the following: white; news; rice; antler; he; she; it; knee; to enter; to walk; to scratch; old; nine; a Himalayan owl; glue; odor; origin; catfish!

Two months of struggling with syntax and syllables went by. One morning Père Hanique informed me that I was to go to Na Hoi — "Oyster Shell Field" — a mission station ten miles from Paksane. I was grateful for the opportunity. Pastoral work, at last!

Immediately I wrote a five-minute homily in Lao, read and reread it until I had it memorized. Saturday afternoon I saddled my horse, carefully tucking my "masterpiece" sermon into the saddlebag. With a slight dig of the spurs, I went galloping down the narrow jungle trail to "Oyster Shell Field" — and my first Lao sermon!

The next morning I went into the sacristy of the tilting bamboo chapel to vest for Mass. On top of the vestments I spotted a scribbled note. It had been left by the pastor the previous Sunday. "Announcement: Request all able-bodied men to help plant the posts for the new church immediately after Mass." And I had no dictionary with me! Great!!! I studied the note for a couple of minutes, hooked a dozen Lao words together which I thought, or hoped, would convey my message to the "able-bodied" men.

After finishing the Gospel, I began my memorized sermon. It was quite an ordeal bouncing up and down the five tones, making sure that my short vowels were short, and the long vowels long. Finally, I concluded my sermon. Then came the announcement — which was unprepared, remember! Struggling through the one-sentence message, I noticed that all of the parishioners — especially the "able-bodied men" — became wide-eyed. Immediately I sensed that I had made a glaring mistake! There was no time now to find out. Turning back to the altar, I continued the Mass.

Back in the sacristy, my server gave me the bad news. I hadn't quite hit the right tonal pitch for *"lak sao,"* which should have meant "to help plant the posts." Instead my announcement went: "Request all able-bodied men to help STEAL THE YOUNG GIRLS immediately after Mass!" I had always believed, "Do your best and God will take care of the rest!" That was one time when he let me down! But I did get ALL of the able-bodied men!

As the days went by, the strange sounds became less and less strange. Lao is an extremely colorful language. Taking a map of Laos, I began translating the names of the cities and provinces. Here are just a few of my notes:

Vientiane	*Sandalwood City*
Luang Prabang	*Royal City of Holy Bang (a pagan god)*
Thakhek	*Foreigners' Shore*
Savannakhet	*Frontier of Heaven*
Tha Deua	*Fig Tree Boat Landing*

Houei Sai	*Clear Creek*
Nong Bua	*Lotus Water Hole*
Pakse	*Mouth of the River Se*
Phong Saly	*Corn Field*
Phou Khao Khouay	*Buffalo Horn Mountain*
Phon Sao E	*Knoll of the Beautiful Girl*

Even the names of people all had meaning. One evening I glanced down the roster of the seminarians. Here are the names of the boys in ninth grade:

Sing	*Lion*
Nouchin	*Chinese Rat*
Sounthorn	*Handsome Man*
Khamsouk	*Happiness*
Khamphone	*Blessing*
Oudom	*Fulfillment of Desire*
Sout	*Last*

This last name, I found, was very common throughout Laos. When the parents deem that this newborn child is their last, very often they will call that child "Thao Sout," namely "Master Last." However, it also frequently happens that "Master Last," in time, has a younger brother or sister!

"Why did your parents give you the name 'Bua'?" I asked one young seminarian. The word meant "Lotus"; thus he came in for a lot of ribbing from his fellow seminarians.

With a shy grin, he answered, "The night I was born, my grandmother saw a lotus flower in a dream. Since she was not a Catholic, she firmly believed that in my previous existence, I had been a lotus flower. Now I was being re-incarnated as a human being. Hence I should retain the name 'Lotus' to signify my ancestry."

The five tones are perhaps the greatest stumbling block for all young missionaries — and all foreigners, as well. These tones are similar to five notes in a scale. A word pronounced on a "do" pitch will have an altogether dif-ferent meaning from the same word pronounced on a "re" or "sol" pitch.

One Saturday afternoon, two American officers from the Military Attaché group drove to Paksane to spend the weekend with me. The main reason they came was to have me translate some twenty short phrases from English to Lao. This, then, was to be printed and placed in the standard U. S. survival kit for Americans flying over Laos.

The translation came easy, for the questions were short and simple. For example:

> "I am an American."
> "Where are other Americans?"
> "I am hungry."
> "Where is rice?"
> "Where is water?"

Then came the important question: "Where is the en-emy? Near? Far?"

My two friends tried pronouncing the translation, *"Satrou, you sai? Kai?"* (high pitched, meaning "far"). *"Kai?"* (low pitched, meaning "near").

Shaking his head, Joe said, "You know, Father, it will be a tragic mistake if I get my *kais* mixed up!"

CHAPTER FIVE

The Dying Monk

CHRISTMAS WEEK in Paksane was filled with great excitement for all of us. Mail arrived! I received sixty-four letters, the first mail since my arrival in Laos nine weeks previously! Years ago in Rome I learned that one of the greatest blessings a man overseas could have was regular mail service. Unfortunately, Laos had not yet been so blessed.

Among the letters was a note from Bishop Loosdregt in Vientiane. After a brief Christmas greeting, he wrote: "Please proceed to Nam Bac as soon as possible. OB [Operation Brotherhood] Hospital personnel request English-speaking priest."

"Where the heck is Nam Bac?" I wondered. I had never even heard of it. Once again I resorted to my trusty Rand McNally Atlas. The name wasn't on the map!

That evening in the refectory, I asked the Fathers if anyone knew how to get to Nam Bac. No one had ever heard of it. Suddenly Père George Kolbach, one of the veteran missionaries of Laos, piped up: "Ah, Nam Bac! Oui! Oui! I walked through Nam Bac on our way to Kunming."

"Kunming?" I thought to myself. "Is the Bishop ordering me to China?"

Père Kolbach had spent many years as a chaplain with the French Army during the Indochina War with the Japanese. "It is the last stop before going into Dien Bien Phu," he explained, "which is some four hundred miles north of Vientiane."

I was relieved! It wasn't China — and it wasn't North Vietnam either! But I wondered how far his "last stop" was from the North Vietnam border!

"The only way you can get there, Matt," said Père Kolbach, "would be to go to Vientiane. Perhaps in the city you can find some transportation for the remainder of the journey. You see, the only time I was there I went on foot," he concluded. Four hundred miles on foot!

After packing a small bag, I set out the next morning for the bus depot. Remembering my trip down, I was not looking forward to the journey. This bus was modern. It had a top on it! But it still had the same movable, or turn-over-able, benches.

By 5:45 a. m., the bus was loaded, and I do mean loaded! Men, women, babies, bundles, and produce for the Vientiane market were stuffed into the ancient truck. So were several sacks of rice, more crocks of the fragrant (!) fish sauce, three live — and large! — sows, and baskets of ducks and chickens.

The veins in the driver's neck bulged as he screamed at his passengers — animal and human — to move back and make room for the endless cargo he was shoving aboard. Since this bus had a top on it, baskets of poultry and a couple of young boys were perched on the roof. The driver and his helper tried to hoist one of the sows up on the roof, but couldn't quite make it! Amid much squealing and oinking, the animal was deposited on the "floor" of the bus atop my feet! With a blast of the horn to clear the street of water buffalos and ducks, we were off for Vientiane.

High noon found us at the ferry landing of the Nam Ngum River, two-thirds of the way to Vientiane. Several trucks were ahead of us, and we were told to wait our turn. We waited all right — three hours! Once on the other side of the river, our driver pushed the accelerator down to the floorboard trying to reach Vientiane before dark. The bus had no headlights!

Suddenly several elderly women in the bus let go with ear-piercing shrieks. The driver slammed on the brakes, the bus skidded and lurched to a wobbly stop. Passengers began leaping over the sides of the bus and running into the thick jungle after six scared, flapping ducks that had "flown the coop" off the top of the bus! Animals, passengers, and one very harassed bus driver limped into Vientiane as night settled over the city.

"There are two ways you can get to Nam Bac, *mon père,*" the Bishop told me over breakfast the next morning. "You can go by jeep to Luang Prabang, some 250 miles from here, and then take a horse or, if you prefer, walk the last hundred miles." With a smile, the Bishop added, "This will take you a week."

I groaned inwardly, but went on to ask, "And what is the other way, Bishop?"

"Well, if you can find a plane, and a pilot, you can fly."

The remainder of the day was spent searching for a plane. By noon I had found Pierre, a veteran French pilot who knew the route and was willing to take the risk.

The next morning at sunrise we rattled down the runway. The plane was the kind I used to make models of when I was a kid, over twenty years before! It was a single-engine plane, which is a nice way of saying we had to fly over treacherous mountains and deep jungles with just one sputtering motor!

We left behind the lush green valley of the Mekong, with its shimmering rice paddies, and headed for the mountains of northern Laos. Mountains, everywhere! Ridge after ridge of jagged, jungle-covered peaks, many reaching over seven thousand feet! These same mountains roll on and on, under the Bamboo Curtain of North Vietnam and China, and up and up until they peak in the majestic Himalayas of Tibet and Nepal.

The vast carpet of green foliage beneath was dotted intermittently with clusters of huts, part of the eleven thousand villages which make up this Kingdom. "So that is how ninety per cent of the people of Laos live," I thought to myself.

The villages on top of the mountains belonged to Meo tribesmen. They usually had only four or five huts. Attached to each clump of huts was a bald, charred spot on the flank of the mountain, sign of the slash-and-burn method that shoves the jungle out of the way to make room for the Meos' upland rice planting. Clinging to the sides of the mountains were the villages of the Kmhmu tribe. These, too, consisted of a few huts surrounded by vast charred areas.

Nudging me in the ribs to get my attention, the pilot gave the "thumbs-down" signal. As he pushed the stick forward, the nose of our shuddering Beaver dipped down abruptly. I watched the altimeter — six thousand feet, five thousand — finally at one thousand feet the pilot eased back on the stick, and the tiny plane leveled off.

When my stomach rejoined the rest of my body, I looked out the window. Noting Pierre's big grin, I realized he wanted to give me a better view of the river villages. For the next twenty minutes we followed one of the wider mountain streams, the pilot skillfully weaving our plane between the mountains towering high above us. These villages were larger, ten to twenty huts. Small patches of gardens were visible along the bank. Several pirogues were moored alongside the villages. Rice fields, water buffalos, all indications of stability. These were not the nomadic *montagnards,* but Lao tribespeople.

The pilot veered off from our river course, gained altitude, hurdled a few more mountain ridges, then swept down to a bouncy landing at what appeared to be a fairly large city. (I found out later that the poulation was almost eight thousand!) We were at Luang Prabang, the royal capital of Laos.

Crawling out of the cockpit, Pierre handed a few letters to one of the soldiers guarding the landing strip. Then, aided by a couple of coolies, he rolled a drum of gas over to our plane. After refilling the tank and stretching a bit, Pierre climbed back into the cockpit. Soon we were airborne again.

Another hour of flying, another hour of towering mountains and thick jungle. Then I noticed the altimeter needle starting to move counter-clockwise. We were getting ready to land. But where? The flaps were down and our altitude was only a couple of hundred feet. But I couldn't see Nam Bac, or even a landing strip. Everything was jungle!

As Pierre steered the Beaver sharply to the left, around a mountain, I saw a clearing. It couldn't have been more than a couple of hundred yards long. Off to the side was Nam Bac — all thirty huts!

As the plane touched down, the pilot pointed to the left. Just off the side of the runway was the wreckage of a C-47. "The French Army was parachuting ammunition and food to our garrison here a few years ago," he explained. "Viet Minh ground fire got them!"

Just as the plane slowed to a stop, I noticed a huge heap of mangled metal on the edge of the dirt strip. Pierre cut the motor and opened the window to let in some fresh air.

"That used to be a bulldozer," he pointed. "They were supposed to use it to lengthen this airstrip." With a shake of his head, he said ruefully, "I told them to put a couple more 'chutes on it when they dropped it from the plane!"

We pulled our gear out of the plane and started walking over to the small village of Nam Bac. A group of villagers, off in the distance, was heading our way. Suddenly I noticed a young boy racing ahead of the group. When he reached me, he said excitedly: *"Khoun Pha! Khoun Pha!* (Revered Father!) Hurry!" As I trotted alongside the boy toward the village, he panted out a story of an old man who was dying and had asked to talk to a Catholic priest. The dying man was a former Buddhist monk!

I spent an hour with the old man. It was obvious that he knew quite a lot about Catholicism. As a boy in the area of Dien Bien Phu, he had learned about the Catholic religion from a friend. His sincerity impressed me.

As I leaned over to check his pulse, his gnarled hand grasped my Oblate crucifix, pulling my face close to his. While I knelt, inches away from his burning eyes, he pleaded with me to baptize him. So, on the shaved head of the former Buddhist monk, I poured the saving waters of Christ's baptism.

Kneeling at the side of the monk's cot, I heard him gasping for air. Suddenly the rasping sound stopped. My first convert in Laos was on his way to heaven! All during that long bouncy flight from Vientiane, I kept wondering why the Bishop was sending me all the way to Nam Bac to preach a mission to only six people. Now I understood!

* * *

"Credo in unum Deum." The rich voices of the six Filipinos soared in unison as we celebrated the High Mass. Their voices were filled with happiness and gratitude. My visit to Nam Bac, and the three-day retreat which I had preached for them, marked the first time their hospital in the hills had been visited by a priest since their arrival two years previously. The one-room bamboo hut which served as their dispensary, ward, and pharmacy, was crowded with the four nurses and two doctors of the Operation Brotherhood team, plus some thirty men and women from the village. Children squeezed in. Even a few dogs attended Mass that morning!

This was the first time that the Lao villagers had ever witnessed a Catholic ceremony. Although I gave them a few words of explanation in Lao before Mass, I'm sure they did not grasp in the least the real meaning of all those Latin hymns and liturgical gestures. However, they knew it was some sort of *sakara* — a ceremony dealing with the gods. Consequently, they were very reverent.

Breakfast was a gay gathering. The villagers, all one hundred of them, gathered to bid me *pai di* (go well).

Afterwards, I hurriedly packed my small bag, all the while keeping a sharp ear pealed for the hum of my Beaver. Pierre had promised to come back to Nam Bac to pick me up the morning of the third day. "Just as soon as the fog has lifted," he had said.

Well, this was the third day — ten a. m. — and the fog had lifted. It was a beautifully clear, sunny day without a single cloud in the sky — and nary a plane in the sky either! "What a beautiful day for flying," I thought, "if only I had a plane to fly in!"

Noontime. Still waiting and listening, I sat down for lunch with my Filipino friends. Again, all of the villagers gathered around the table to join in the meal and bid me farewell. Several more hours of waiting. Four p. m. Pierre couldn't possibly make Luang Prabang or Vientiane before dark. No one ever flew at night, for none of the landing strips had lights. An instrument landing was out of the question. Vientiane was the only city in the entire nation that had a control tower, and even that closed when the sun went down!

My fourth day in Nam Bac came and went. Then the fifth, sixth, seventh, and still no Pierre! Had he forgotten me? Had he crashed into the side of a mountain? There was absolutely nothing I could do. Telephone or telegraph links with the world outside the Nam Bac Valley just did not exist. The nearest telephone was a couple of days walk due east — in HANOI! I wasn't quite that desperate yet!

Mid-morning of the eighth day, we heard a faint hum. The small group of villagers stopped chattering. Everyone tensed and listened. Yes, that was Pierre all right!

Minutes later the dilapidated Beaver touched down on the airstrip, whirling thick clouds of dust into the sky, and into our hair, too! Pierre stopped the plane, swung the tail around and taxied over to where I was waiting. Clumsily he crawled out of the cockpit.

My impatience and curiosity got the best of me. "Pierre, where the hell have you been the past five days?"

With a sheepish grin, he gave me a couple of weak excuses: having a headache, being real busy.... But his bloodshot eyes and red nose gave me the REAL answer. Poor Pierre had got tangled up with that Mekong firewater again. A five-day binge!

CHAPTER SIX

Struggle for Survival

"NERNG, SONG, SAM, SCI...."
Back in Paksane again, I bounced up and down the Lao scale. The tones were getting easier, and I attacked the study of the language with zest. The sooner I mastered Lao, the sooner I could begin pastoral work in earnest.

Pushing the books aside and lighting my pipe, I took a breather, reflecting on the enormous differences between life in the mountain villages, and life here in the valley of the Mekong. The contrast was unbelievable! Up north, the Meo, Kha, and Yao tribespeople were more stocky, ruddy, hardy, more vigorous, and more energetic. This is due to the fact that the air is nippier, their Chinese ancestry more recent, and the very fundamental fact that it's darn hard to grow one's living on the side of rocky mountains!

Here in the Mekong Valley, life paced itself more slowly. The languid climate, the swaying palm trees, and the fertile delta soil meant that one didn't have to slash away and burn down a whole mountainside every three years. For decades the rice fields had been passed along from one generation to another. It was the ancestors (God bless them) who had cleared these rice fields in years gone by. All the Lao had to do today was plow, plant, and harvest. Rivers produced an ample supply of fish for the ordinary family. The people were not forced by nature to be nomadic. Their villages were stable and permanent; their houses sturdily built. The average Lao family would invest in a few coconut trees, banana trees, some manioc, planning ahead to make life easier in the years to come.

For the people of Nam Bac, even a simple drink of water meant hours of struggle and toil. Climbing up and down a mountainside to reach a valley river or spring made water a luxury. For the Lao of the delta, the nearby river provided an ample supply of water for every need of the family — bathing, cooking, and drinking.

My days in the hills had fired me with enthusiasm to get to work. But they also had made me more grateful for the things I had heretofore taken for granted. For example, one of the greatest contrasts between life in Laos, and life in civilization, struck me every night as I lit my kerosene lamp for a few hours of study before "lights out." As I grumbled to myself about "primitive" living conditions, I had not realized that I had begun taking even the kerosene lamp for granted. Up in the mountains, kerosene is a luxury, the last word in "better things for better living." Lighting a lamp in Nam Bac meant using a precious reserve of fuel which had been acquired after a ten- or twenty-mile walk to the nearest large-size village where one could purchase a quart of kerosene for an exorbitant price. What little could be brought into the villages of the valley had to be transported by horseback — or "human" back — many hours, even days, up the sides of the mountains.

Yet even in the valley, life was hard. I was beginning to be seasoned, to understand the realities of life in the missions. In the snug enclosure of the Oblate Generalate in Rome, I had pored over the archives, looking at countless photographs of native huts, tribesmen, Asian farming implements, etc. Now I realized what a totally ignorant impression I had formed!

A photo of a shabby bamboo hut in a mountain village had impressed me with its obvious poverty. But I had never before felt the aching muscles and oozing blisters that resulted when one tried to climb the mountain to get to that poor hut, as the inhabitants of those villages did every day of their lives. Mealtime in Rome meant sitting at a clean table, stashing away a meal which I now knew was literally "fit for a king," although by Western standards it was modest and simple. Now I knew that "to eat" in Laos meant to stalk a bird or a monkey through the jungle for hours, to spend weeks planting what resulted in a few grains of rice. A hot cup of coffee was unknown, and a glass of contaminated water a triumph of hours of walking and lugging a leaking bamboo pail.

A missionary priest is formed, not at the moment he says *"fiat"* to God's call to the religious life, nor at the moment when his hands are anointed with sacred oils on the morning of ordination. A man becomes a missionary the day he shares the precious polluted water of his people, the day he squats on the floor of their shabby huts to share their simple meal of rice and fermented fish, the day he lights his kerosene lamp and says *"Deo gratias"* for the flimsy flame that flickers feebly as the mosquitoes dive and dance around the heat of the lamp. He may be a missionary in his mind, but until his body and heart join him in battle, until his conscience is acutely aware and genuinely grateful for the gifts of God formerly taken for granted — until that day, he is not really a missionary!

Reams have been written about undeveloped countries: the lack of industry, education, agricultural progress, social development. But very little is ever recorded about the ingenuity of the people of those "undeveloped" countries.

Long before the rest of the world ever acknowledged the existence of these mountains and valleys, the people of Laos were at war, battling nature to carve out their existence. Somewhere in history, ancestors found the means of hacking away a jungle to plant rice. They tamed the elephants and boars. They tilled their fields, using crude, hand-carved plows. The women designed their looms to weave thread which became yards of cloth to cover their bodies and protect them against the cold. Kettles, crocks, dishes, everything needed to hold, carry, or cook food was devised, designed, and made by hand. Even firearms and gunpowder were devised and made at home.

The villagers learned to utilize everything. They didn't wait for foreign-aid programs to survey the countryside and begin to ship in tons and tons of metal monsters and miracle gadgets. Bamboo, vines, strips of wood, woven grass, coconut husks, herbs, shells, weeds — became roofs, walls, pots, buckets, skirts, and food.

They even licked the "credibility gap" with local advertising! The news-media problem created by the lack of radios, television, billboards and newspapers was solved. The town-crier system!

Riding a bicycle or horse up and down the main (and only!) street of a village, shouting through a homemade bamboo megaphone, the "crier" would convey the latest news to the populace. No doubt the guy who thought this up somewhere back in the fifteenth century was the forerunner of Madison Avenue! The "news broadcasts" would be interspersed with commercials advertising the latest product for sale: a water buffalo; a litter of pigs; a trapped

wildcat; a chunk of deer meat; a basket of mangoes....
"Stop by at Ling Fo's hut for a tasty side of water buffalo — special today!" (Because tomorrow it would be ran-
cid and inedible!) The fee: a couple of kips (pennies) per
announcement!

The struggle for survival in Laos has gone on for centuries, and it will be a couple of more centuries before
things get much better. Life in the valleys is an unending
struggle. Some win.... Others.... Nay Ling was one who
didn't win.

As I walked through the village of Paksane one afternoon, I spotted an old derelict, seemingly dead, propped
up against a palm tree. Bending down, I felt for his pulse.
It was thready and weak. Lifting the frail body up and
over my shoulders, I headed the half-mile back to our
dispensary.

Nay Ling had been chased from his village three years
earlier. He was an opium addict. In order to earn money
to buy rice and opium, he began selling water. Drawing
it by the bucketful from the Mekong River, he stumbled
from hut to hut. The kips he earned went to buy less and
less rice, and more and more opium.

For three long years, the homeless addict sold water,
smoked opium, and slept in sheds. Finally one afternoon
his body collapsed under the punishment. As he drifted
in and out of consciousness, I stayed at his bedside. When
he was coherent, I would speak to him about God, preparing him for death. Late that night he asked to be baptized.
Thus I chalked up my second Lao convert, an opium addict!

Several days later we buried Nay Ling in the cemetery
at our seminary. In a small plot of land shaded by towering *kok bok* trees, a hand-hewn cross marks his grave with

the simple epitaph, "Nay Ling." For me, however, that cross said more, much more. It told of a young man who willingly had entered the struggle for survival. He fought hard, but he just couldn't win. Despair drove him to opium and to belief in the spirits. And he was just one of millions in Asia who entered the struggle for life — and didn't win.

CHAPTER SEVEN

Mission in "Flowering Falls"

"IT'S TIME we put you to work, Father," said the Bishop. "Let's see how much Lao you've learned." With these words I received my first resident assignment, assistant pastor in the village of "Flowering Falls," Ban Keng Sa Dok, fifteen miles down the Mekong River from Paksane. Confessions, baptisms, instructions, sermons — my three hundred words of Lao would be hard-stretched!

Ban Keng Sa Dok was larger than the ordinary Lao village. It had some eight hundred inhabitants. Otherwise it was typical in style: no electricity, no running water, no stores. I was something of a celebrity because of having the only time-telling instrument in the entire village — my wristwatch.

The small church was "modern." The walls were made of woven bamboo and plastered over with mud. Once upon a time, someone had whitewashed the church. Now, just a few small splotches of faded white were still visible. The roof was covered with wooden tiles which the villagers had hewn out of the jungle. The floor was hard-packed dirt. The pews — there weren't any! Ironically this church was called St. Peter's! The St. Peter's of Ban Keng Sa Dok was a long way from the St. Peter's of Rome. But in Laos it was the envy of all the other villages.

61

"Khoun Pha! Khoun Pha! Ma ni de!" As soon as I heard the frantic yell of my catechist, I raced out of the rectory. Two enormous water buffalos were locked in combat. Snorting, pawing the dust, the bulls charged headfirst into one another. Backing away, they roared their anger and charged again, and again. The villagers were clustered together in a semicircle, fascinated with the excitement.

As the fight progressed, one bull began to overpower the other. The loser decided to quit. Spinning around, he galloped away from the larger bull — and headed toward St. Peter's! As the people, and I, ran after him, yelling and shouting, trying to steer him on another course, he became even more frantic. The poor animal was so terrified, and galloping so fast, he didn't alter his course a single degree. "Hrrumph!!!" He slammed broadside right through the wall of the church. With a thundering bang, mud, plaster, and bamboo splattered in all directions, as the bewildered buffalo tore through the church.

I picked my way through the debris and ruefully thought: "The least he could have done was to enter like everyone else through the front door, which stood wide open. But no, he had to open another exit in the wall."

Snorting and bellowing, the exhausted bull was led out through the wall as the other bull stood docilely by.

*　*　*

The days sped by, filled with Mass, confessions, preparing sermons. Quickly the unfamiliar Lao syllables adapted themselves to my Texas tongue, and I immersed myself in village life. The high spot of the day was the few hours after supper in the evening. Walking through the village, welcomed and greeted by everyone, followed invariably by a platoon of grubby kids fascinated with the towering height of *Khoun Pha,* I picked up many stories and tales of the history of Ban Keng Sa Dok.

The inhabitants of Ban Keng Sa Dok belong to the Muoi tribe. Until the end of the nineteenth century, the tribe lived peacefully in small villages scattered through the mountains of northern Laos. About 1880, during one of the frequent Lao-Siamese wars, a band of Siamese soldiers captured most of the people and sold them as slaves in Siam.

The missionaries across the river in Laos, seeing the horrible treatment these Muoi were enduring, began buying the slaves. Bringing them back into Laos, they would liberate them. The ex-slaves were so overwhelmed by the priests' generosity that many of them asked to be baptized Catholic. Today all of the descendants of these Muoi slaves in the Ban Keng Sa Dok area are Catholics.

During my two months in the village, I spent many interesting evenings squatting on the floor around the fire, listening to the gripping tales the people had heard from their parents and grandparents.

Nang Boun remembered very distinctly. With her five elder brothers and sisters, she was helping her parents harvest the annual rice crop. "It was my sixteenth rice crop," she recalled. "Suddenly we saw clouds of smoke billowing from the jungle ahead. Our village was on fire. We all jumped from the oxcart and ran back toward the village. A group of Siamese soldiers leaped out in front of us. An arrow pierced the throat of my father. He died instantly. The rest of us were captured, our hands tied behind our backs with vines, and we were led to the camp just outside our burning village.

"The next morning my three elder brothers were taken from the camp. I never saw them again. Day after day, the number of prisoners increased. Several weeks later, about two hundred of us were led from the camp and taken to Siam, three weeks' walk. There we were sold as slaves, that is, those of us who were still alive. I was the last of my family to be put on the market. I'll never forget the afternoon my mother was sold."

Tears came to Nang Boun's eyes as she recalled her mother being led away. "I do not know where she was taken, or how and where she died. I spent the next three monsoon seasons as a slave working in the rice fields of a Siamese landlord.

"One afternoon a white man appeared in our village. I remember him very well, for he was the first white man we had ever seen. He was dressed in a long black robe. We were told that he was in the camp to buy slaves."

With a smile she went on: "After bartering for a good price, the white man bought fifteen slaves. I was one of them. He took us across the Mekong to the Laos side of the river, then several kilometers inland. We were amazed at the kind treatment. The white man in the black robe led us to a clearing in the jungle, where he had started a small village. He called the village 'Ban Keng Sa Dok.'

"When we arrived in the village, he announced: '*Yiou ni bo mi kha* (Here there are no slaves). You are free,' he said.

"Together with the other villagers, the white man helped us build houses, plow our fields, and to know the one, true God. I was free! At the end of our first rice harvest, he asked us to contribute as much rice as we could spare. He was going back to Siam to buy, and free, more slaves."

Shortly after Nang Boun told me her story, she died. As I recorded her death in the parish register, I noted the few brief lines:

Name:	Nang Boun
Date of birth:	Unknown
Place of birth:	Unknown
Father:	Boun Tin — murdered by Siamese bandits in Tran Ninh
Mother:	Sao Kham Luen — captured by Siamese bandits in Tran Ninh, taken to Siam, sold as slave. Fate unknown
Date of Baptism:	Unknown (records burned by Vietnamese Communists in 1953)
Place of Baptism:	Ban Keng Sa Dok

I closed the register. Nang Boun was the last of the original slaves. But the village of Ban Keng Sa Dok remains, a monument to the kindness and sacrifice of the white man in the black robe.

CHAPTER EIGHT

Filling the Gap

THE WORD "URGENT" was written in big red letters. The envelope, arriving late in 1957, was tattered, damp, and covered with fingerprints. Ripping it open, I read: "You are needed in Ban Khang Si. Leave immediately. Stop at Vientiane en route. Will give more details. (Signed) E. Loosdregt."

The terse letter from the Bishop had taken more than a week to reach me, traveling from Vientiane to Paksane on the *loat me,* then by pirogue from Paksane to my mission at Ban Keng Sa Dok.

I tossed my few belongings — shaving gear, couple of shirts, a pair of pants, and breviary — into my rucksack and headed for the pirogue which had brought my urgent communiqué from the Boss. After a day of jogging along on the venerable "mother truck," I arrived in Vientiane and headed for the Bishop's house.

After months of isolation in the boondocks, I was hungry for news of the "outside world." The Bishop quickly filled me in.

The Royal Lao Government and the Pathet Lao (Communist Party) had signed a pact declaring the two northernmost provinces of Laos, Phong Saly and Sam Neua, re-attached to the Vientiane government. After the fall of Dien Bien Phu and the Geneva Treaty which followed in July 1954, these two large provinces had remained under

Communist control. The latest agreement specified that the two battalions of Pathet Lao troops defending these provinces would be incorporated into the Royal Lao army. The Pathet Lao political leaders would be given posts in the Lao Government!

This pact, in essence, was just another Communist ruse. By granting the Royal Lao Government the right to hoist the Lao flag once again over these two chunks of territory comprising some fifteen thousand square miles, the Communists obtained the legal means of incorporating over one thousand Communist military and political leaders into the very core of the Lao Government structure. Never ones to miss an opportunity, the Communists had spent their years of occupation well. They had infiltrated Communist cadres into the provinces and compiled well-documented dossiers on all the leaders, and potential leaders, of the provinces.

Many of the villages scattered through Sam Neua province were Catholic. However, when the Communists took over in 1953, the priests were forced to take refuge in the jungle. Father Tien, a zealous young native priest, had been captured and killed. For the past five years, these neophyte Catholics had been deprived of the sacraments and the consolation of the Church.

Shortly after the signing of the pact, Bishop Loosdregt boarded one of the first planes destined for Sam Neua. A few days of scouting the area convinced him of the dire need for priests throughout the province, despite the risks involved! Bordering on North Vietnam, the Sam Neua mission would be one of the most dangerous ever undertaken by the Church in Laos. In an area heavily infiltrated with Communist agents and without roads, communications, or river traffic, the men of Sam Neua would be totally and completely isolated! The only way in, or out, would be by plane. If a missionary needed surgery or any important medical care, he would just have to wait — and HOPE — that a plane would make it in and carry him the four hundred miles back to Vientiane.

Seeing the stifled emotion on Bishop Loosdregt's face as he told me the details of the Sam Neua assignments and described the decisions he had made for the reopening of this vast mission territory, I understood the tremendous responsibilities of a Bishop, especially in the missions! This simple, kindly man was living with the choice of giving his men a "life or death" sentence. The obstacles, the known — and unknown — dangers, made it quite probable that few of these priests would ever return alive.

Added to this personal burden was the incontrovertible fact that only the very best men could be assigned. They would have to know the dialects of the area: Meo, Kha, Thai Deng. They would have to have ample medical experience, not just to treat the people, but also to keep themselves alive. They would have to be sturdy, have enormous stamina and physical reserves to withstand the hundreds of miles of hiking that would be required of them. They would have to be spiritually strong in order to penetrate the barriers of paganism, animism, and witchcraft permeating the entire province.

So Bishop Loosdregt prayed — and wrote — to Fathers Bertrais, Subra, Brix, Rancoeur, Charrier, Gaillard, Bouchard, Loison. To complete the team, he added two lay missionaries, both Canadians. The letters sent to each of the priests were essentially the same: "Dear Father: We need you in Sam Neua. Please find the means of getting there as soon as possible." A simple note, a couple of lines, and destiny was set in motion.

One problem solved, the Bishop found himself confronted with another. The assignment of the special team to Sam Neua left a number of critical mission stations vacant in other parts of the country. The only permanent solution would be to obtain more priests from Rome, France, America. But it would take months just to find them, and years to train them. Meanwhile, the rest of us would have to do our best to plug the gaps!

The gap I was assigned to fill was Khang Si in Xieng Khouang province. That night after supper, Bishop Loosdregt took me into his office. By the light of a flickering candle, we talked well into the night.

To get to Xieng Khouang, and eventually from there to Khang Si, I would have to go by road. It would take six, eight, ten, or more days. But always an even number of days, for the road was one way! On the even days of the month, the Xieng Khouang-bound traffic moved. On the odd days of the month, the Vientiane-bound traffic moved.

In the United States this would be unheard of, naturally! Imagine the Pennsylvania Turnpike being one way — one day! On Monday you could drive from New York to Pittsburgh. On Tuesday you could drive from Pittsburgh to New York. Too bad if you wanted to go to New York on Monday, and Pittsburgh on Tuesday! But the Alleghenies are not the Himalayas, or even the foothills of the Himalayas. And above all, stateside turnpikes are not hacked through the wilds with machetes.

The Vientiane-Xieng Khouang road couldn't quite be called a turnpike, but we in Laos did appreciate it immensely. It was our only contact with civilization, which couldn't be said for many other parts of Laos. That dusty, narrow strip of chuckholes to us meant salt, rice, nails, cement — anything which we could truck in — and everything we needed to survive!

The newly arrived Americans always went into culture shock when informed of the "travel schedule" for the Laos turnpike. "Why wasn't the schedule changed every week? Why didn't they build a two-way road?" One trip on the road soon put an end to their logical questions and solutions. A single day of bouncing in and out of chuckholes, with dangerous curves and steep drops down the side of the tilting highway, made them grateful for the schedule of one day travel, one day rest. Both the passengers and the truck needed a day to recoup and muster up the courage to travel another day of kilometers.

I signed on with Nguyen-Van-Thong as his first, and last, passenger. His Lao assistant was Kham Di. Every truck always had an "assistant" along to help repair the truck (on alternate days), watch the cargo (every night), and ride on top to call out potential danger spots ahead in the road.

Thong's truck wasn't exactly the last word in travel. As a matter of fact, I marveled that it still had any go in it at all. But Thong was very proud of it. It was an old French "4 x 4," which he had "obtained" from the French Army upon his discharge after the battle of Dien Bien Phu.

"Ah, *Khoun Pha*," he said as we were bouncing along the morning of the first day, "I loved my truck very much. I became very attached to it."

And, I thought, "You were so attached to the truck that it followed you right out of the Army. That day the French Army scratched one corporal — and one camion!"

Kham Di was grandly installed atop the cargo, which I later learned was drums of gasoline. "Not very encouraging if we happened to have an accident or turn over," I thought.

The six-day journey passed with only a few minor mishaps. At one particularly sharp curve in the mountains, we listed to starboard, and over the side of the truck rolled a drum of gasoline. Thong slammed on the brakes and we lurched to a stop. The drum bounced its way down the flank of the mountain, crashing into a glorious burst of flames.

Scratching his head, Thong muttered, *"Bo pen nyang!"* Throwing the truck into gear, he drove on, unconcerned and unworried. After three days of driving and bouncing, with a day in between to allow the Vientiane-bound traffic to pass, and Thong to tighten the bolts on his *cher camion,* we arrived in Khang Si.

CHAPTER NINE

The Rhode Island Reds

PUSHING ASIDE MY TIN CUP and plate, I opened my medical kit. Life in Khang Si had quickly evolved into a standard routine. Four a. m., out of the sack and down on my knees for morning prayers. Then a half-hour of meditation, followed by Mass. A quick breakfast of whatever was left from the night before — usually sticky rice, a few cold vegetables, washed down with water — and sick call would begin.

The Kha villagers of Khang Si were warmhearted people. They quickly welcomed me into their hearts and homes. The Kha huts were built on stilts, like the Lao down in the valley. However, when they got around to building a hut for the priest, I suppose they ran out of stilts. My house was smack on the ground! If there had been an architectural design contest in our village, my rectory would have won the prize for simplicity! All it had were six posts driven into the ground, woven bamboo tacked on the sides, and thatch laid on top.

A flimsy bamboo partition, part way up, cut the single room into two areas. The first half served as living room, dining room, dispensary, library (for my six books), catechism room, and chapel. The back half served as storage for food, kerosene, work tools, and — oh, yes! — a small bed squeezed into one corner! I didn't need a kitchen, for two families had been appointed by the village elders to bring me my meals, wash the dishes (all two of them), and take my laundry down to the creek once a week.

At the seminary in Rome, as soon as the dishes from one meal were washed, we would set the table for the next meal. So, on one of my first nights in Khang Si, after washing my plate and cup, I set out the dishes for breakfast. The next morning as I sat down at the table, I found the dishes and table covered with a thick layer of dust that had sifted down through the thatch roof. During my entire stay in Khang Si, that dust, and the mosquitoes, were my two biggest crosses!

Every day started with sick call. The peace and calm of a leisurely breakfast were always shattered by the whimpering and crying of sick babies, and the soft chatter of patients gathering outside my door. My one room served as dispensary, clinic, and examining room.

Drawing on every bit of knowledge I had gleaned during my months at Santa Rosa Medical Center, and my one year of med training at the Knights of Malta Hospital in Rome, I treated countless hundreds of patients. Word quickly spread that Ban Khang Si had a "doctor." I dug in and scraped out infected cuts, dosed stomach worms, bathed the stumps of leprous hands and feet, delivered babies, vaccinated, inoculated, sewed, and treated.

One day the villagers carried in a man who had been mauled by a bear. The jungles of Laos abound with wild animals — bears, tigers, elephants, wildcats, cobras, and pythons. I stitched together the jagged gashes on his body and shot him full of penicillin and tetanus vaccine. His scars wouldn't be pretty, but at least he was in one piece again.

* * *

Khang Si had quite a reputation throughout Xieng Khouang province, not just because it had a *Khoun Pha Mah* (priest-doctor), but because of its clean water. In fact, it had been nicknamed "Ban Nam Saat," or "Clean Water Town."

The villagers of Khang Si formerly dipped water out of the small stream which ran through the town. This water served all needs: drinking, cooking, washing of clothes and bodies, watering of buffalos and ducks. At any hour of the day, one would always find women squatting on the bank scrubbing their clothes and children, ducks paddling merrily in the shallow water, and people dipping that same water to be used for drinking and cooking.

My predecessor, Père Subra, then decided to apply a little preventive medicine to the many cases of "G. I's." Following the stream up into the hills, he found its source about a half-mile from the village — an abundant spring of crystal-clear, icy cold water gushing out. Gathering all the elders together in his hut, Père Subra outlined his plan to pipe drinking water directly from the spring to the village. The elders were enthusiastic.

The next day everyone — fathers, mothers, children — began chopping lengths of bamboo to serve as pipe. To protect the "piping system" from marauding water buffalos and pigs, it was elevated several feet from the ground. To reduce the number of steps the people had to carry their drinking water, feeder lines of bamboo tubes were connected to the main bamboo pipe, thus furnishing outlets in various locations of the village.

Three days later, the Khang Si Water Works were blessed. It was incredible how a missionary, and a few lengths of bamboo, plus many hands could wipe out so many stomach problems and unnecessary deaths.

* * *

Some twenty miles across the mountains a group of six Americans, all members of International Voluntary Service, had a small experimental farm. As I mulled over an idea which had been "bugging" me for quite some time, I decided to propose it to the other Americans.

Rolling some sticky rice in a banana leaf and filling my canteen with water, I grabbed my old baseball cap and set out. It was a beautiful day. The sun was high in the cloudless sky, and there was a balmy breeze.

Six hours later, I reached the IVS camp. After searching out Clyde Searles, who was in charge of that particular IVS operation, I told him my story.

"Clyde, I want to launch Operation Rhode Island Red! Can you help me?"

"Sure, Father. Just tell me what you've got in mind."

Lighting my pipe, I began to tell Clyde about Khang Si and of my desire to better the poultry production. Khang Si had the same problem as all the other villages of Laos — no real chickens! Sure, every family had a few chickens fluttering around the huts. But they were a scrawny, wild breed which laid pigeon-sized eggs, that is, when they DID lay! Twice a year cholera epidemics would wipe out most of the flock, plus a few buffalos and other animals.

"Let me see what we can do for you, Father."

A few days later, a roaring Land Rover rolled into Khang Si. Behind the wheel sat Clyde, a big grin spread all over his face.

"This came up on today's flight from Vientiane," he said. I opened the parcel. Lo and behold! Vials and vials of anti-cholera vaccine!

"And that ain't all, Padre," Clyde said. Walking around to the back of the Land Rover, he pulled down the tailgate and hauled out a crate. Six hefty Rhode Island roosters! Clyde came through in real American fashion.

The six roosters were posted in hen coops throughout the village. Within months we had healthy little half-breeds twittering proudly up and down Khang Si's main street. The only problem I had in "Operation Rhode Island Red" was preventing the villagers from making soup out of the roosters. "Breeding purposes only!" I had to keep reminding the people. Though I dared not admit it, there were many days when I, too, was sorely tempted to nab one of the roosters for my pot. Whenever I sat down to one of my meatless meals (and there were many!), my mouth would water for a Southern-fried drumstick.

* * *

One of the Articles in the Oblate Rule states: "Every member of the Society will make a day of recollection each month." So, obediently, I would pack my breviary, sleeping bag, and a few odds and ends in my rucksack, and once a month hit the trail for Xieng Khouang mission station. It was an enjoyable, peaceful walk through the jungle. Crossing over the hills, I could get a beautiful view of the seven- and eight-thousand-foot peaks scattered throughout the area.

Seven hours of brisk walking would bring me into Ban Pha, a Thai Dam village where Père Leroy had his mission. I would spend the night with him, and we would set out together the next morning for the city of Xieng Khouang, a walk of another eleven hours. In this sector, as in most of Laos, rarely did one estimate the distance between two points in miles or kilometers. It was generally in "hours of walking."

Although it cost me four days of hiking, I always looked forward to the monthly retreat. In addition to the spiritual "shot-in-the-arm," it afforded an opportunity to spend the day with the other priests, seven in all, gathered together from throughout Xieng Khouang province. As we sat around the table, puffing our pipes, and exchanging ideas and experiences, it was the closest any of us came in those days to a quasi-"civilized" life. We were all isolated from the world, from our own native milieu, from companionship and intellectual stimulus. Like a pack of gabby gossipers, we were hungry for news.

Xieng Khouang — and Retreat Day — were to me synonymous with the outside world. Since there was no mail delivery in the villages, all mail would be delivered to the Catholic Mission in Vientiane — 250 miles away. There our procurator would bundle the letters and send them to Xieng Khouang whenever a plane was headed in that direction. When the retreat ended and I again hit the trail back to Khang Si, my bundle of precious letters stuffed inside my shirt, I often reminisced about those mornings back home in the U. S. when we would complain because the postman was a bit later than usual in reaching 212 El Monte! I would never complain again!

Père Leroy was a husky, dynamic thirty-year-old missionary. The distances he used to walk each week were staggering. One day these distances and his meager diet got the best of him.

I had arrived late in the afternoon on my monthly walk to Xieng Khouang. He was jolly as always, but I noticed a pallor in his complexion and a slight slowness in his actions. He moved as if his body were a dead weight.

"Are you ill?"

He shrugged it off with a smile. "It's just a little diarrhea."

The next morning, despite my objections, he insisted on going to Xieng Khouang for our retreat as usual. After an early Mass, we set off down the trail. For the first few hours we kept up a fairly brisk gait. On these jungle hikes, the cardinal rule is: "Don't ever be caught on the trail at night!" For us missionaries, it was the "first commandment" — one never to be forgotten!

After the first hour or so, Père Leroy began to slacken. Soon we were stopping to rest every fifteen minutes. By mid-afternoon I realized we would never make Xieng Khouang by nightfall. In fact, it was evident that Père Leroy wouldn't make Xieng Khouang at all under his own power.

I stretched my sleeping bag beneath a tree and told him to rest and wait for me. Breaking out into a fast trot, I double-timed it down the trail. After several hours, I arrived at the mission station.

Out of breath and numb with fatigue, I mumbled a few words to one of the priests, and grabbed the mission's two horses. Racing back up the trail, I reached Père Leroy. I boosted him onto the horse, and we headed back to the mission. Fortunately, there was a French army doctor in Xieng Khouang. It turned out that poor Père Leroy had not only diarrhea but also a severe case of amoebiasis and malaria!

CHAPTER TEN

The Emerald Mystery

IN BAN BAN, two long days' walk due east of Khang Si, was a small Operation Brotherhood (OB) hospital. The six-man medical team, all Filipinos, were doing a tremendous job under difficult circumstances. Word was sent from Vientiane asking me to make a side trip to the OB Hospital in order to give the Filipino team a three-day retreat.

There are only two plateaus in Laos, a land of valleys and mountains. One is called the Bolovens Plateau, in the southern portion of Laos near the Cambodian border. The other is the Plain of Jars in Xieng Khouang province. To get to Ban Ban meant that I had to walk across the entire length of the Tran Ninh Plateau, the famous Plain of Jars.

Nestling in a bowl of mountains, the Plain is laced with tiny streams gushing out of the surrounding mountains. The edges of the bowl are formed by majestic, jagged peaks reaching seven and eight thousand feet into the sky. Clusters of bamboo huts on stilts dot the Plain, generally along the banks of the small streams.

The Plain derives its name "Jars" from the several acres of crudely hewn stone jars which litter the area. Four to six feet in height, and up to three feet in diameter, the jars hold a centuries-old mystery which has never been solved.

To Lao and *falengs* (foreigners) alike, they are a fascinating untold story. Some historians claim that the chunks of stone were originally funeral jars, or coffins, as we would say. (The pallbearers must have been giants to carry these coffins!) Others claim that the jars served for the storing of rice.

How many hundreds or thousands of years these jars have been there, no historian dares to guess. Who made them? Why? How did they transport them? The mystery remains unsolved. The only point of certainty is that the jars had to be transported, for there is no stone in the area surrounding the Plain.

The Plain of Jars nestles between the Gulf of Tonkin and the Mekong Valley. To the north are the mighty Himalayas of China; and far to the south, the Gulf of Siam. With its strategic location, the Plain has been used as a battlefield for centuries. To hold it, to control it, meant one could hold — and control — a kingdom, an entire nation, or more!

Sweeping down from Yunnan, the Chinese came first. Then the Vietnamese poured over into the plain from Tonkin and Annam. The Siamese fought for this strategic emerald sod. The Khmers fought their way up from Cambodia in a futile attempt to seize control of the Plain.

The hapless villagers saw their huts burned, their possessions sacked, their families taken into slavery or murdered on the spot. Heaps of broken red brick, remnants of pagoda walls, are mute symbols of a prosperous and happy past.

To me, the Plain of Jars will always be one of the most beautiful sights in Asia. Now it is littered with the debris of battle — the skeletons, bones, empty shell casings, bomb craters, and pockmarks of the fierce fighting with the Communists which has centered around the Plain in recent years. But that day the Plain was serene — a quiet sanctuary of beauty which paid tribute to the skill of its Creator.

On the far end of the Plain was the famous "PDJ" (Plaine des Jarres) airstrip. It wasn't very wide or very long. Leveled with picks and shovels by countless coolies, the dirt strip was one of the busiest in all of northern Laos.

Purple shadows streaked across the Plain as I arrived at "The Bungalow," at the edge of the airstrip. Parked in front were a couple of tired jeeps (left behind by the French after the war), and a half-dozen small airplanes, ranging from the clumsy Beaver to the sleek Beechcraft. On one side of the Bungalow were a few bamboo huts, and two flimsy metal hangars used only during the monsoon rains.

I had heard much about this famous Bungalow! I wasn't over the threshold many minutes before realizing that everything I had heard was true. It looked like a replica of "Lily Mae's Tavern" of the Wild West days back in the States.

Meandering through the door, I saw five or six Frenchmen sitting at the bar. A buxom waitress came up and invited me to "join François at the bar." I soon realized that François was one of the bosses. His job was to check out every visitor, not that there were that many!

The ground floor of the two-story frame structure consisted of a bar (well-stocked with the finest French wines and liquors) and a couple of tables for dining. Upstairs were accommodations for "visitors" — a couple of third-class rooms, and a dormitory.

Washing facilities were a gasoline drum outside the kitchen door. However, just outside that same door was a baby tiger on a leash and a huge black bear in a cage. I didn't brush my teeth that night! The outhouse, too, was just outside that door. During the night I used the front door!

The residents of the Bungalow were very obliging. They would fly anything for you: passengers to Vientiane, opium and gold to Phnom Penh and Saigon. Although they called themselves a "passenger airline," practically all of their business consisted of dropping large containers of opium at prearranged drop zones hacked out of the jungle just outside of Saigon or Phnom Penh, or even in the Gulf of Siam, where the containers would be fished aboard waiting junks.

The Bungalow provided its residents with all the comforts of home — gold for money, opium for dreams, booze for pleasure. But these men were good to me, and to all of the missionaries who would stop by for a meal and a night's rest. There was never any question of a bill. After all, these soldiers of fortune were devout French Catholics!

The next morning I said Mass on a rickety table in my room. Then once again, I hit the trail for the last half of my hike. The Operation Brotherhood team in Ban Ban received me warmly, in typical Filipino fashion. We converted a corner of their small living room into a temporary chapel. A folding surgical table served as an altar.

As I lay in bed that night in the clean antiseptic atmosphere of the OB Clinic, I couldn't help comparing it to my previous night in the PDJ Bungalow!

CHAPTER ELEVEN

"Oblate Killed by a Tiger"

THE SPRING OF 1958 marked a rapid increase in the number of conversions, especially in the northern provinces of Sam Neua and Xieng Khouang. The number of catechumens among the Hmong and Kmhmu tribes of these provinces was greater than at any time in the 250-year history of the Church in Laos.

Consequently, Bishop Loosdregt was transferring as many missionaries as possible up north. But the old mission stations couldn't be abandoned. So it meant that the number of missionaries had to be spread out over an even larger territory. In the spreading-out process, I received a new assignment: Nong Veng.

Once again I found myself in the Valley of the Mekong, this time 107 miles east of Vientiane and four miles north of the Siamese border. During the dry season (November — April), my post could be reached by jeep. However, during the remainder of the year, the monsoons turned the last eight miles into a swamp. Eight miles of water, mud, and bloodsuckers! The only way I could travel through this swamp was on horseback or foot.

Nong Veng was a typical Lao village. Back in the latter part of the nineteenth century, a group of men chopped out several hundred acres of jungle. In the middle of this newly cleared area they erected their bamboo huts. The remainder of the field encircling the huts was planted in rice. A large swamp nearby served as an excellent hunting spot. Wild animals of all sorts would come out of the jungle at night to drink from the swamp. Thus the village was named Nong Veng or "Water Hole."

From the time of its founding to the day I arrived some seventy-five years later, the village had not changed at all. Oh, sure, more huts had been built to accommodate the population increase. But that was it! Civilization had never reached Nong Veng. The people still plowed their rice fields with water buffalos and hand-hewn wooden plows. Bamboo shoots dug in the jungle, greens pulled out of the water hole, lizards, frogs, monkeys — any animal they could shoot or trap in the forest — supplemented their diet of rice.

Open firepits in the corner of the huts served their cooking needs. Torches made of dry wood pulp soaked in resin tapped from the *mai khang* tree provided light. A mat woven out of *theury* leaves and stretched on the bamboo floor was bed. There were no stores, no hospitals, no electricity, no running water, no roads. Nong Veng was literally just a clump of huts plunked down in the middle of the jungle.

God, in his infinite wisdom, keeps young missionary priests too busy during the initial stages of their apostolate to observe keenly the incredible change of milieu. The constant demands on spiritual and physical strength, the pressing needs of the people he is helping, preclude the missionary's being too concerned with himself. He is unconcerned that the water in his cup may be polluted. A long day's hike through the jungle and all water tastes good! And when the aching body is stretched out on the *theury* mat at night, he swiftly drifts off to sleep without remembering that there are such things as clean sheets and soft beds in other parts of the world.

When I was in the seminary in Rome, and even after my ordination, I had a very incomplete (or perhaps "naïve" would be more apt) idea of the duties of a priest. I thought they were limited to the spiritual domain: preaching the Gospel, administering the sacraments, saying Mass. However, in Laos, I quickly learned from experience that a priest must also be the village medicine man: general practitioner, pediatrician, surgeon, obstetrician, and dentist.

As in my previous assignments, sick call played a major role each day. I would average a minimum of three hours each morning doctoring the sick. The illnesses were pretty much the same — malaria, stomach worms, vitamin deficiencies, leprosy, tuberculosis, snakebites, pneumonia, eye and ear infections, pregnancies, tooth extractions. Many a time I wished for a real M. D. at my side, or better still, wielding the scalpel! When I get to heaven I'm going to award my guardian angel an M. D. and a D. D. S. for all his valuable assistance.

One night shortly after I had arrived in Nong Veng, I was reciting Lauds in my bamboo hut. I had just moved the prie-dieu for the fourth time since starting, trying to find a dry spot. The wooden shingles that roofed my hut were excellent until the monsoons began. And that particular evening's monsoon was having no pity whatsoever on my frail shingles!

Suddenly a torch appeared in the doorway. There stood two men, drenched and tired. I didn't recognize either of the bronzed faces.

Ling, adjusting the machete on his hip and holding the torch to one side, quickly began: *"Khoun Pha! Khoun Pha!* My wife is dying. Please come quickly."

"What village do you come from?"

"Ban Na So Ma — two hours' walk away." Ling went on: "This evening when I returned home from planting rice, I found my wife unconscious. She has had a high fever for several days, chills, too. Several times she asked for you this afternoon. But our four small children were the only ones at home...."

High fever, chills.... MALARIA! That dreaded plague of the tropics was reaching for another victim. This would be my third case in twenty-four hours!

Syringes, nivacine, holy oils, ritual were quickly wrapped in my waterproof sick call bag. As I tucked the pyx with the Sacred Host in it into my jacket pocket, I thought, "Dear Jesus, get ready for a wet two hours."

The monsoon howled as the three of us plodded barefooted through the slush and mud and blackness. We had gone about one hundred steps when Ling paused and pointed: "Tiger killed water buffalo here two weeks ago." I felt like telling Ling that that was absolutely the wrong thing to say at a time like this! Pushing the thought out of my mind, I trudged on.

Thirty minutes later our flickering torch indicated the trees. We were across the rice field. A couple of miles of jungle lay ahead. Phong, who was walking ahead of me, unsheathed his razor-sharp machete. We might be needing it now!

On and on. Soon we were at the Nam Kha Din river. Outside the monsoon season, it's only a dry creek bottom — but now! The stream was only forty or fifty feet

wide, but the swift current was mercilessly hurling bamboo poles and broken limbs along with uprooted trees
past us. Ling and Phong stopped abruptly! *"Khoun Pha,
the bridge has been swept away!"*

I pushed aside the thick bamboo. The bridge was not
of the "Golden Gate" variety. It had been just a couple
of logs tied together with vines, wide enough for a man
to walk across. But now there was nothing! We would
have to swim!

I took the pyx containing the Holy Viaticum from my
pocket and tucked it inside my sick call bag. Holding
the bundle with one arm, I waded in. Three steps and the
water was over my head. Fortunately no logs were coming
downstream, only a few long poles of bamboo. Pushing
them aside, I swam on. Scrambling up the muddy bank,
I slipped, and started to fall back into the stream. Ling
grabbed me by the collar of my jacket and dragged me
ashore. Soon we were tramping through the jungle on
the other side.

Sopping wet, shivering from the cold as the wind
howled through the jungle, we trudged on. Ling stopped
abruptly!

"Khoun Pha, tiger was here!" In the flickering light,
I could see the fresh tracks. "Oblate missionary killed by
tiger!": I could visualize that headline flashing over the
news wire. "Dear Lord," I prayed, "please don't let that
headline be published — at least not until after the sick
call!"

On and on we walked. The rain had stopped, the
monsoon wind spent. All was quiet — very quiet! Ling
pulled up short, throwing his arm out flat, stopping me
in my tracks.

"Berng! Berng! (Look!)" A couple of steps ahead of us was a long *tham than,* a grey and black-striped member of the cobra family. It was coiled tightly, ready to spring. Gingerly we stepped off the trail, giving wide berth to the *tham than* as we circled around him.

Eleven fifteen p.m. Tiredly we climbed the ladder of Ling's bamboo hut. Sieng, his wife, was still alive, perspiring heavily. Her pulse was weak. Immediately I gave her an injection of nivacine and camphor oil. "I anoint you . . . ," I began as I administered the Last Sacraments.

One a.m. Sieng was breathing more regularly. Pulse stronger, fever going down. We said another rosary.

Two a.m. Another vial of nivacine. Respiration and pulse a bit more normal.

Three a.m. With Phong, I began the long trek back to my village to say Mass.

Six a.m. Back in my hut, vesting for Mass, I felt tired. My feet were sore and blistered, I had a gash on my right knee, suffered when I had stumbled. But I was happy. I had cheated malaria of another victim!

CHAPTER TWELVE

Black Magic

HOW MANY PEOPLE died unnecessarily in Laos! This thought haunted me constantly ever since I arrived. Only a small percentage of the inhabitants of this section of the world had the advantage of medical care.

One morning I had a sick call in the village of Na Hua Phou, two miles from Nong Veng. The woman had a serious attack of pneumonia, aggravated by an entire colony of ascarids.

As I was preparing the syringe for a penicillin injection, the woman admitted that she had never had an injection or taken a pill in her entire forty-one years! In fact, no one in her family had! As a result of this lack of medical care, her husband had died at the age of thirty-six, and four of her six children had died before the age of two! No wonder that the average life-span in Laos was twenty-seven years. No wonder that fifty per cent of the children died before they were one year old, and another twenty-five per cent died before the age of five!

How many hundreds of people I treated each month, I really couldn't say. I never counted them. For one reason, I did not have time. For another, it really didn't matter. The important thing was to save as many lives as possible.

Perhaps the greatest cross a missionary has is not the food, or the isolation, or even the danger. Rather, it is a feeling of inadequacy. So much to do — and only two hands with which to do it! So many people in desperate need — and so little to give them! Each time I saw the fever of a malaria patient go down, I thought of the thousands and thousands of less fortunate scattered through these primitive jungles. I thought of those who at that very moment were dying of malaria or pneumonia. I thought of that large chunk of humanity who did not have a doctor, or priest, or quinine.

I suppose that is the real reason a missionary does not count the number of lives he saves. He is more concerned with the lives of those he is not reaching, but should, and perhaps could, if he tried a little harder. That is why each morning, as I made my meditation before Mass, I would beg Almighty God to make "today" a bit more successful than "yesterday."

Nong Veng was good basic training. During my months there, I was seasoned — and shocked! I witnessed medical procedures which had never been mentioned in the antiseptic halls of Santa Rosa in Texas and San Carlo in Rome.

Take the case of Leuan, aged ten. Energetic and playful, he was just like a ten-year-old boy anywhere in the world. Leuan and his parents lived a couple of huts down the path from my rectory. One afternoon, as Leuan was returning from the rice field with his parents, he saw his younger sister eating *mak kham* (tamarind berries). He asked her for some. A typical eight-year-old girl, she answered curtly, "If you want some, climb the tree the same as I did."

Leuan did. In trying to collect more than his sister, he went out too far on a limb, and suddenly came plummeting down flat on his back! People came running from all around to the unconscious boy.

One of the *me thaos* (grandmothers) immediately had the remedy. Scurrying back to her hut, she plucked three different types of herbs which were hanging from a rafter near her bed. Quickly she mashed them into a pulp. Dumping the concoction into a bowl, she filled it with urine. Carrying the bowl back to the unconscious boy lying under the tree, she forced it down the hapless lad's gullet. Minutes later he regained consciousness. Three days later Leuan was back working in the rice field with his parents.

I later asked a number of villagers what they really thought of this remedy. Unanimously they all agreed that it was the miracle drug of the century. "Maybe so," I thought to myself, "but what century?"

Multiple was the variety of these local miracle drugs. Certain berries, tree bark, leaves, roots, were all used. Sometimes they were boiled and drunk, as in the case of a high fever or a pain in the belly, regardless of whether the cause of the pain was stomach worms or a ruptured appendix! Other times they were pounded into a paste and often mixed with other ingredients such as buffalo dung, betel juice, ashes, and then rubbed into the open sore. Tiger teeth, pounded into a powder, had an exceptionally high curative power. Undoubtedly some of these remedies did have medicinal value but most of them were based on superstition and witchcraft.

Summoned to a pagan village some four or five miles from Nong Veng, I examined my patient, a young woman. Semi-conscious and with a temperature of 104 degrees, she tossed and turned on her straw mat. My suspicions were confirmed immediately: another case of post-delivery infection so very, very frequent in these jungle villages. I gave the patient a hefty injection of penicillin and promised her that I would return the next morning.

As I was repacking my medical bag, another man entered the hut. Bowing very politely *à l'orientale,* he introduced himself as Nay Chop, the *mah pao* ("blow doctor"). He immediately pulled his "medical bag" out of his back pocket, a filthy rag containing several different sizes and colors of "cud." These he stuffed into his mouth and began masticating vehemently.

Accumulating a mouthful of saliva, the *mah pao* began spraying it on the patient, over the entire length of her body. In order that the healing power of the "miracle drug" might penetrate to the innards of the patient, the spray must come in direct contact with her skin. Hence the feverish woman had been bared — ninety-nine percent of her, that is.

While the mouth was doing the spraying, Nay Chop's feet were performing rapid, rhythmic dance steps. His feet pattering a staccato tap on the floor of the hut, his hands in a constant state of gesturing and gesticulating, the *mah pao* worked himself up into a state of catatonic frenzy. Stopping only to cry out several weird incantations, which sent chills up and down my spine, he would bend low and spray the weird-smelling saliva juice over the woman's body.

The following morning I returned to my patient's village to check her condition and give another shot of penicillin. I kept this up for almost a week. Soon she was up and taking care of her three small children again. As a

token of appreciation, her husband gave me a chicken —
live! Since chickens, and all kinds of domestic animals,
were rare in this part of the jungle, this was a sign of great
gratitude on the part of the family. I've often wondered
if the Blow Doc got a chicken, too.

CHAPTER THIRTEEN

Danger at Salt Lick

"SUAY! SUAY!"

Awakened by the shrill, piercing shriek, I leaped to my feet. *"Suay! Suay!* (Help!)"

I recognized the voice. It was my cook, screaming for help from her hut, just fifteen steps from mine. I ran to the door of my hut. Seeing nothing in the black night, I shouted, *"Mean Yang?* (What's up?)"

Her answer came back. *"Ya su ma! Ya su ma!* (Don't come!)"

I was bewildered. Here was my cook yelling for help, and, in the next breath, shouting at me not to come! Then, in the faint moonlight, I noticed a movement under her hut. Suddenly a shadowy form lurched out, dashed across the open area between our huts, and leaped over the bamboo fence.

Within seconds, most of the villagers, including me, were grouped around my cook. Trembling violently, she related the episode to us.

She had been sleeping on the floor of her hut with her three children next to her, as usual. Suddenly she was awakened by a loud roar in the pigpen just below her floor — and bed! As she peered down through the cracks in the woven bamboo floor, she looked directly into two glistening eyeballs less than a foot below her. A tiger! That's when she shouted!

The frightened but hungry tiger was not going to abandon his meal. Grabbing a large sow, he raced between our huts, then leaped over a three-foot-high fence, all the while carrying 150 pounds of meat in his jaws!

Nong Veng was noted not only for its tigers, but also for its elephants, tame and wild ones! There is no animal in Laos more feared by the people than the wild elephant. And rightly so! There is no protection against him, no weapon to stop him, not even the native muskets. Often the bullets would merely deflect off the elephant's hide. Or, if the bullet would penetrate the hide, it would lodge in one of the many inches of tough muscle and flesh protecting the elephant's vital organs.

Our elephants had phenomenal olfactory faculties, too. One day Père Jacques Brix and Père Armand Clabaut, who were stationed at Ban Pak Kadin, the mission next to mine, needed some meat. Picking up their rifles, they headed for Nong Kera (Salt Lick) — a water hole noted also for its saline properties. Nong Kera was very popular with the wild animals of our area. All species and varieties would meander along the edge of the pond, licking the soil to acquire the nitrogen chloride which their systems required.

When they arrived at Nong Kera just before dark, the two priests climbed up into their small lookout high in one of the tall trees. This lookout consisted of just a couple of planks nailed together in a fork of the tree. It wasn't much, but it was certainly less painful — on parts of the anatomy, that is — than spending the night perched on a limb.

The wind was coming from the right direction. The bright moon afforded excellent visibility in the clearing around the water hole. A perfect night for bagging a deer or a wild pig.

Foxes, wildcats, young does, came and drank, but the Fathers held back, hoping for something with a little more meat. Then, suddenly, out of the black jungle stepped a huge buck. Père Clabaut, who was on watch, nudged Père Brix, who was dozing next to him. Silently, slowly, they raised their rifles into position. As they waited breathlessly for the deer to graze a bit closer, they heard a sharp cracking of brush in the jungle behind them. Another animal was coming! They listened. The cracking and crunching became louder, and nearer! Suddenly out stomped three huge ELEPHANTS!

Pausing at the shore of the water hole, the three elephants erected their mammoth trunks, and gently gyrated back and forth like huge radar screens, sniffing any danger signals. At the first sound of the elephants, the deer that the two hunters had in their sights scampered back into the safety of the jungle.

The three elephants drank their fill. Again gyrating their "radar systems" in the air, they clumsily tromped back into the jungle. After a few minutes, judging that there was a safe distance between themselves and the elephants, the two scared hunters eased themselves down the tree and hightailed it back to the safety of their village.

Three nights later the two priests went back to try their luck again. They found the huge tree in which they had their lookout, flat on the ground, UPROOTED! The night after their visit to Nong Kera, the elephants had returned. Scenting the presence of a man from the previous night, they vengefully snooted the tree over to the ground. When the two priests saw their lookout, and the entire tree, smashed to the ground, they thanked God that the wind had been with them!

CHAPTER FOURTEEN

The Chickens' Church

"Sssss." Looking up from my Lao books, I peered through the dim shadows of my hut. For the last few minutes I had heard a soft hissing, on and off, on and off. "Sssss. Sssss." There it was again! I had to find out what it was.

Padding softly around the room, I lifted my sleeping mat. Nothing there! Maybe behind the curtains covering my shelves of supplies. No, nothing there either! "Just my imagination!" I thought.

As I turned back to the table, more than a little annoyed with myself for being such a "nervous Nellie," I glanced casually at the open window above the table. The overhang shutter was propped open with a stick to let the cool night air into the stuffy room. A COBRA! Coiled comfortably atop the window ledge, the four-foot length of black velvet swayed slowly back and forth, emitting an occasional soft hiss.

Backtracking carefully, all the while staring eye to eye with my black visitor, I reached the corner of the hut where my rifle was propped against the door. Slowly I lifted the rifle, took aim, and fired. The sinuous black body popped into the air as the slugs of my M-1 tore through. As it landed on my table, atop my Lao notebook and papers, the snake glistened like a black jewel in the

flickering light of the kerosene lamp. Gingerly sliding my
rifle under the body, I tossed it out the open window.

The favorite outdoor sport of my brother, Hank, and
me had been hunting rattlers and moccasins in the rocks
and mesquite of our one-hundred-acre farm in Texas. Despite the admonitions of Mom and Dad, we had great fun
bringing in our burlap sack of snakes to display to our
friends, and to show off our skill as "great white hunters."

Perhaps I had acquired wisdom, as well as age, in the
years since. Whatever the reason, I had gained a healthy
respect, and a natural fear, of the deadly black cobras which
abounded in Tha Ngon. As they crept up from the river,
they represented a constant threat of instant death!

After I had been eight months in Nong Veng, the
Bishop assigned me to Tha Ngon, a small village fifteen
miles north of Vientiane. I found the new mission station
to be a real challenge. While it had the usual number of
problems, it also had compensations. With the number
of Americans in the capital increasing rapidly, the Bishop
had decided to send me to Tha Ngon, instructing me to
spend at least one Sunday a month ministering to the spiritual needs of the English-speaking Catholics in Vientiane.

On one of my trips into Vientiane, I paid a visit to the
Bishop, to say "hello," and to ask for a hundred bucks!
The small frame rectory-chapel at Tha Ngon, with its
wooden shingle roof, was spacious enough. But with the
advent of the monsoon season, I was kept busy bailing
water out of the house. The leaky shingles had to be re-
placed. So I took my problem to the Boss.

"Sorry, *mon père*," he said; "we have no money."

I couldn't believe it! An entire diocese, covering half the country of Laos, and not even enough money to repair the roof of a small chapel!

"Don't be concerned, Father," the Bishop continued. "I'm sure you'll find a way to fix the roof." With a friendly smile, the Bishop waved good-bye.

Turning over the possible alternatives in my mind, I discarded begging, for the people didn't have any more than I had. I spent the next few days mulling over my problem of finances. "Canon law says that a priest can't go into business," I thought to myself. "But it doesn't forbid a priest to raise chickens."

Searching out a good pagan Chinese friend of mine, I haggled a credit deal for two hundred Leghorn and Rhode Island Red hens. The next step was to find customers — with money, that is!

Ringing the doorbell at the home of Bridget and Colonel Edgar Sanders, Deputy Chief of US/PEO (Program Evaluation Office), I broached the subject. Bridget had adopted me as a "kid brother." Their house quickly became home for my one-night visits to Vientiane. A hot shower, a good meal, and a soft bed were standing by, waiting for me, whenever I could come to Vientiane.

"Bridget, how would you like to peddle eggs for me?"

Never one to be thrown by a wild idea, she quickly answered: "Sure. How many do you want me to sell?" Explaining my goal of raising a hundred dollars to repair my church, I worked out an arrangement with Bridget that I would deliver eggs to her house once a week. She, in turn, would sell them to the other American wives, collect the money, and keep the books.

Business flourished! The roof fixed and the walls repaired, my mission at Tha Ngon grew rapidly, thanks to the fertile hens.

One Sunday morning I tied ten dozen cartons of eggs on the back of my Honda and headed for Vientiane. Rounding a corner on the outskirts of the city, I hit a patch of gravel. The motorcycle stopped cold, but I kept on going! Flying through the air, I hit the dust and rolled over several times. More worried about the eggs and motorcycle than myself, I dusted off my cassock and remounted. Everything seemed to be in good shape, so I continued on my way.

A week later I found myself in Mahosot Hospital, my leg hoisted above my head in traction, with a cast running up to my hip. At the time of the accident, my only injury, so I thought, was a bloody knee. Two days later, the entire leg was swollen and festered, with my knee twice its normal size. Met by the French doctor with a barrage of epithets attesting to my stupidity and lack of care, I was firmly ordered to bed for a minimum of six weeks. When I protested, the doctor told me in no uncertain terms that I could choose between six weeks in bed or amputation of my leg at the hip. From that day on, I had as healthy a respect for motorcycles as I had for cobras.

CHAPTER FIFTEEN

City of Sandalwood

I WAS IN THA NGON for one year. It was a very happy and successful year. Although it is never possible to judge the spiritual good accomplished, I looked back with satisfaction. My baptismal register showed I had baptized eighteen children and eleven adults. Moreover, at Ban Na Kang, fifteen miles farther north in the mountains, I had twenty-five young men under instruction. If these pagan men persevered, their families, and probably their whole village, would be converted. The little bamboo chapel I had constructed in Ban Na Kang, and those twenty-five catechumens, were my pride. This totally pagan area had never before even heard the word of God mentioned. I'm sure that many holy nuns prayed hard for me during my twelve months in Tha Ngon.

On December 18, 1959, I reported to Bishop Loosdregt in answer to his summons calling me into Vientiane.

"I am reassigning you, Father," he said. "I want you to build another parish here in the city, one for Lao and English-speaking Catholics."

Thrilled and excited at the prospect of becoming the pastor of a large parish in Vientiane, the "City of Sandalwood," I hung onto his words. "This must be a very extensive parish, serving many needs of the people. You must build a sizable church, a rectory and, of course, a school."

I was amazed at the enormity of his plans. " . . . a hostel for homeless boys," he was saying, "and a carpentry shop to provide jobs for the people of the neighborhood."

Here was a science completely new to me. In the seminary it was philosophy and theology; in my post-seminary training it was medicine and mechanics; and now I needed architecture and engineering. The next few weeks I pored over sketches and drawings.

The church would accommodate three hundred people and be designed so that in the future it could be converted into a parish hall and auditorium. The hostel would provide a home for twenty-five orphaned boys, plus living quarters for married Lao catechists. The rectory would have offices, meeting rooms, and, on the second floor, sleeping accommodations for four priests. Over the refectory would be a set of rooms which would serve as space for printing and translating catechetical material into Lao. The school was to be a three-story unit, with classrooms for five hundred students.

The plans finished, I hesitantly delivered them to the Bishop. He glanced at the rough sketches and designs, then said, *"Très bien! Très bien!"* I was relieved and proud. This was my first (but I learned later, not my last) building baby.

"When do you want me to start, Bishop?"

"As soon as possible!"

"Right away?"

"Right away!"

"But what about the money?"

"That's your problem!"

One hundred and twenty-five thousand dollars! How to raise such a sum? Not even my fertile hens could produce enough eggs to bring in that much! Back in my bedroom-office, I meditated, not on the mystery of the Trinity or on the theological virtues, but on how to raise some cold, hard cash — quickly!

This center would be tremendously important for the Church in Vientiane, and Laos! It would serve as the meeting point for all the Lao Catholics coming from the mountains to Vientiane, and also for the English-speaking — Americans, Filipinos, British — whose numbers were increasing rapidly in the city.

St. Joseph will provide! Pulling my portable Smith-Corona out of its case, I began pounding the keys. Everyone I knew in the U. S. — family, relatives, kissin' cousins, chance acquaintances, schoolmates, nuns, friends — heard the news of my new assignment and my plea for help. As the letters continued to flow outward across the sea to the States, the first replies were beginning to arrive in Vientiane. Nickels, dimes, a dollar here, two dollars there — the generous hearts of America shared in the excitement and anticipation that this new parish would indeed become a reality.

At dinner one night in the home of Evelyn and John Hackett, I mentioned the warm response of the people at home. Some thirty Americans were present for one of Evelyn's famous "get-togethers."

"Don't leave us out of it, Father," John said. "After all, it's OUR church you're trying to build!" Glancing at his wife, John continued, "I don't have any cash — but take my car! We'll be leaving soon, and I'll worry about transportation when I get to my new post."

John Sullivan, Consular Officer of the American Embassy, pulled out his checkbook and wrote a generous offering.

Bob Barnack emptied his wallet and pockets, spilling his leftover change into one of Evelyn's cooking pots: $82.00 in greenbacks, 400 Lao kips, 45 Thai baht, and 8 Filipino pesos. Bob proudly displayed his empty pockets and remarked, "It's a good thing I don't have to take a taxi home!"

I returned to my rectory that evening enriched with $2,500 in cash, one Ford Fairlane, and a heart full of gratitude for the generosity and warmth of these friends.

The goal of $125,000 was still a long way off, but we had made a good start. It is customary in Laos for all Buddhist temples to have an annual *boun*. The fiesta produces fun — and money — for the support of the wat (temple). Since the Catholic Church tried to adopt as many of the traditions of the country as possible, we adopted the *boun*.

Word spread quickly among the Lao Catholics of the city. Soon they were dunning the merchants, Catholic and pagan alike, for prizes, display booths, and games. The *boun* lasted three nights. A team of Thai boxers was flown up from Bangkok for an exhibition match, courtesy of Major Son Lay of the Royal Lao Army. Air tickets to Hong Kong were donated for a raffle. Air Vietnam came through with a round-trip ticket to Saigon. Mrs. Ky-Quan-Thanh and Dr. Ky-Quan-Thanh, the Vietnamese Ambassador to Laos, donated a sewing machine and several beautiful Vietnamese lacquer paintings.

The Filipinos of OB and ECCOIL (Eastern Construction Company in Laos), not to be outdone, came through with typical Latin zest. Happy, fun-loving people, they organized monthly bingo parties which soon turned out to be the "night of the month" for Vientiane.

Enthusiastic over the success of their bingo parties, the Filipinos added entertaining shows, skits, and contests. A glass eater displayed his skill; costumed toreador dancers entertained; and a beauty contest chose "Miss Philippines of Vientiane." The triumphant shout of "BINGO!" brought a choice prize — and money into the coffers of the Notre Dame Building Fund!

On April 1 — of all days! — work began on the first building. I had chosen Pioneer Construction to handle the actual building work, for it was headed by an American, Charles Duffy. Chuck had been very helpful to me and, besides, he had the only real construction team in Vientiane. Although he himself was not a qualified builder, having come to Laos a few years previously after being a bulldozer operator in Okinawa, he had a good crew and they worked fast.

We had quite an international group. There was Oja, a Korean architect. Kenji, a Korean, and Nick, a Filipino, were chief foremen; Dat, a refugee from North Vietnam, was chief carpenter; Liu, a Chinese, was in charge of the masons; Som Chan was chief of the many, many Lao coolies. And the whole team was building a Roman Catholic church, pastored by an American, in the Buddhist Royal Kingdom of Laos! Real ecumenism!

The days and weeks passed quickly. This was an entirely new kind of apostolate, thrilling and exciting. In a totally different environment from the past years spent in the jungle, I readjusted myself to the new challenge. No longer did my days begin with three or four hours of sick call. Instead they began — and ended! — now with a new kind of activity, organizing a big city parish.

The success of any parish depends not so much on the ability or dedication of the pastor as on the spirit of the congregation. The priest has the prime responsibility for animating and uniting the members of his flock. Making Notre Dame a success depended not on Duffy and his concrete block-making machine, nor on my knowledge of theology and Catholic doctrine. It depended on my gathering a nucleus of dedicated Lao parishioners who would serve as the core of the parish.

The importance of the role of the laity has been a basic concept of the Church from time immemorial; this basic idea existed long before Vatican Council II. Within a few weeks I had my crew of laymen organized. Among them were Mrs. Khan Kap, a dedicated convert whose husband was a major in the Lao army; Mrs. Espanet, an elderly Lao, the widow of a Frenchman shot by the Japanese during World War II; Khamven, and his young wife, Tiansamone, who was secretary to the Prime Minister.

Construction moved ahead, and the five buildings of Notre Dame parish began to take shape. Eager and excited, we made plans for the official dedication on December 8, the feast of the Immaculate Conception.

One evening in early August, I was having dinner with the newly arrived American Ambassador, Mr. Winthrop Brown.

"How's the situation?" I asked. "I hear a *coup d'état* is brewing."

Shrugging his shoulders, the Ambassador responded: "Oh, no! Everything is stable. My men keep me informed daily, and they assure me there is no cause to be concerned."

I returned to my concrete blocks and steel rods, comforted by the reassuring words of the Ambassador. Less than one week later all hell broke loose! And my beautiful church was smack in the midst of it!

CHAPTER SIXTEEN

How To Capture a Nation

AUGUST 9, 1960, was a fateful day for Vientiane..., and the world!

I awoke with a start. Jerking back the mosquito net, I reached for the lamp. Was it really a rifle shot I had heard, or had I been dreaming? I sat on the edge of my bed and listened. Five seconds passed ... ten seconds ... then more shots. Plenty of them! M-1's, machine guns, carbines! They were coming from the prison lookout tower across the street from my rectory.

"Another prison break," I thought.

More shots. *"Yout! Yout!* (Stop!)," shouted the gunmen.

It must be a general prison break, I thought. Last month three convicts had escaped, but there were not this many shots then. Looking out the window, I could see nothing — nothing but night and rain. More shots rang out. My watch told me it was 3:05 a. m. I tucked the mosquito net snugly back under my kapok mattress, and picked up my rosary. As I lay there, bursts of machine gun fire punctuated the words. "Hail Mary, full of grace, ... pray for us sinners ... at the hour of our death."

The next morning after Mass, I walked through the narrow streets of the city. Usually at this hour, the many Chinese and Vietnamese shops which lined Vientiane's streets were bustling with customers. But this morning most of the shops were still boarded closed. Except for a few pedestrians and an occasional *sam loh* (three-wheeled bicycle taxi), no civilians were out that morning. But the city was far from being deserted!

Paratroopers, members of the Second Battalion of the Royal Lao Army, were everywhere! They were armed for combat: steel helmets, camouflage uniforms, jumping boots, hand grenades and ammunition strapped to their waists, carbines and machine guns in firing position. They were guarding the banks, post office, radio station, government ministries, airport, army camps, all the principal street intersections.

Mortars and small cannons, were set in firing position at strategic corners. Dozens of large tanks and armored cars rumbled through the city. Jeeps with light artillery mounted on the back were cruising about, patrolling the streets. Vientiane, the capital of Laos — the quiet, peaceful city slumbering on the banks of the Mekong — had been captured by internal rebel forces!

The capture of the city was a smooth, well-planned operation. At three a. m., two jeep loads of paratroopers jerked to a stop in front of the sentinel guarding the main gate of the Phone Kheng army camp. A rifle shot rang out! Paratroopers rushed to the barracks of the camp commandant. He was immediately arrested, before he could even pull up his mosquito net!

The shot at Phone Kheng was the signal. ZERO HOUR! Shots were relayed from post to post. Bursts of machine gun and carbine fire riddled the thick blackness and monsoon downpour throughout the entire city.

General Sounthone, of the Royal Lao Army, was awakened by the burst of a hand grenade against his bedroom wall. Two bazooka shells whistled through the house. While plaster was still falling in the dining room, the paratroopers rushed the house. One sentinel was fatally wounded, three more seriously injured, and the General arrested. Mission accomplished!

Fort Chinaimo, the armored corps training center, was more difficult to capture. Consequently twenty paratroopers were dispatched to "do the job!"

"Communists coming! Communists coming!" they shouted, as they sped past the bewildered, sleepy sentinel. Rushing on to the Colonel's hut, the rebel lieutenant pounded on the flimsy bamboo door. "Pathet Lao (Communists) attacking Vientiane! Man the tanks!"

The Fort Commander began shouting orders. Soon six tanks were ready for the "Communists." Two paratroopers climbed aboard each tank to mount the cannons. The rebel lieutenant then announced, "Fort Chinaimo is now to be turned over to the Revolutionary Forces!" With the rebels' 75's staring them in the face, the dazed Royal Lao troops could do nothing but surrender.

The siege of the Lao Engineer Corps camp was comical, but sad. At 3:01 a.m., a jeep pulled up to the sentinel. A soldier approached the guard and politely asked him for his rifle. The weary sentinel thought it was a bit early for the change of guard, but he was not going to object. Standing at attention in the heavy monsoon downpour was not comfortable. The sleepy sentinel gladly passed his rifle to the kind soldier and happily tramped back to his barracks, and bed. Ten minutes later a raging major stormed into Barracks 104-B.

"Corporal! Why aren't you on guard?"

The dazed corporal innocently and nonchalantly told the story. The angry major shouted back, "Hell, man, you just surrendered our camp!"

* * *

"Who is Kong Le?" That question was repeated over and over again by the stupefied population of Vientiane. "Who is Kong Le? Why did he start a civil war in peaceful little Laos?"

It was not many hours before we found out who Kong Le was. His name and voice soon became familiar to all of us in Vientiane. During the first five hours, Kong Le issued seven communiqués! They were broadcast over Radio Vientiane at ten-minute intervals. They were printed and distributed from jeeps and tanks, even dropped from Beavers and DC3's.

"LAO PEOPLE, RISE UP! RISE UP! NOW IS OUR OPPORTUNITY FOR REAL FREEDOM. USE THE FREEDOM GIVEN TO US TO CARRY ON THE WORK OF THE REVOLUTIONARY GROUP. HERE IS OUR OPPORTUNITY. RISE UP! RISE UP!

"BROTHER LAO, FEAR NOTHING! HELP EACH OTHER — EVEN IF IT MEANS SACRIFICING YOUR LIVES. DO NOT FEAR THE TRAITORS. HELP ALL LAO TO UNDERSTAND THE UNDERHANDED METHODS AND CRUEL ACTIONS OF THOSE TRAITORS AMONG US WHO WOULD SELL US TO AMERICA!"

General Phoumi Nosavan, commander-in-chief of the Royal Lao Army, was in Luang Prabang that fateful day.

Upon hearing of the *coup d'état,* he immediately began organizing his troops for a march on Vientiane. It would literally be a "march," for tiny Laos had only a handful of DC3's and Beavers, and most of them were based in Vientiane.

Monsoon rains had made all roads to Vientiane impassable, bridges had been washed away. Slush, one and two feet deep in many spots, caused even the most powerful troop carrier to bog down. The only way for troops to reach Vientiane was by foot. And they came by foot!

Two battalions started walking from Savannakhet, four hundred miles to the south. Another battalion began the march from Luang Prabang, 250 miles to the north. Two companies of paratroopers, training in Thailand, were ordered to be ready to launch a countercoup in Vientiane.

When would the countercoup troops reach Vientiane? Heavy street fighting was expected to take place. Tension in Vientiane, among rebels and civilians alike, mounted day by day, hour by hour. The 7:00 p. m. to 6:00 a. m. curfew was rigorously observed. Even during the day, motorists, cyclists, and pedestrians were constantly halted and searched.

Food became more and more scarce. As panic set in, food prices doubled and quadrupled. All roads bringing supplies to Vientiane were blockaded.

August 19, 1960 — 450 American dependents were evacuated by Air America planes to Bangkok, Thailand. A few days later, all the dependents of the Vietnamese Embassy staff in Laos were evacuated. Thousands of Filipinos, Chinese, Indians, and Thai, suitcases and baskets bulging with all the earthly possessions they could carry, fled across the Mekong River to Thailand.

On August 22, the feast of the Immaculate Heart of Mary, I was working in my office. Hearing a car stop, I went outside and greeted John Sullivan, a tall Bostonian, the American Consular Officer in Vientiane.

"The situation looks grave," John said. "The Royal troops will clash with the rebels any day now — in fact, any minute. It will probably be a bloody battle for everyone in Vientiane. The Ambassador has commissioned me to advise you to evacuate immediately. The American Government can still guarantee your evacuation to Bangkok."

"Thank you, John," I replied with a smile. "Tell the Ambassador I'm very grateful, but it's out of the question."

John burst out, "Damn it, Father! This will probably be your last opportunity to get out. If you stay in Vientiane, you'll run a great risk, even probable. . . . "

He didn't have to finish. Both of us knew what could happen to all foreigners, especially American missionaries, should total civil war break out.

"Thanks, John," I said. "But I can't leave these people, not now!" As John walked outside and gravely climbed into the Embassy Ford, I did not realize that within only a few weeks machine gun bullets would be spraying my church, mortar shells would be landing in my rectory yard, huge tanks would be parked in the school playground, and enemy troops would seek refuge in my not-yet-completed new school!

* * *

To stop General Phoumis' troops, Kong Le sent an SOS to the Lao Communists who had been hiding in the thick jungle. Naturally, the Communists readily agreed to assist! Guerrilla attacks, sparked by Communist soldiers, broke out throughout Laos. The Reds and the Royalists clashed at Paksane, one hundred miles northeast of Vientiane. Forty-eight hours of shooting and shelling, and Paksane fell to the Communists.

At five a. m., on September 18, 60mm. mortar shells crashed into our block. Three landed on our front lawn. Like a foolish American, I watched the raid from the window of my rectory. The next morning chunks of shrapnel were found lodged in the wall just inches from where I had been standing!

On Tuesday, December 13, I had just finished my rice and dried fish. We had begun rationing our precious stores of food, trying to make them last until life got back to normal. Suddenly a deafening blast, then a shrill whistle over the rectory. One hundred and five mm. cannons! Then a second, a third. . . . It was Phoumi who fired first, but it was only a question of seconds before Kong Le had his 105's, 120mm. mortars, tanks, and machine guns ripping through Vientiane. Shells and shrapnel dropped everywhere. By four o'clock, Phoumi's assault troops had pushed from Fort Chinaimo to the center of the city — right up to my church!

For the next thirty-six hours, my church, rectory, and nearly completed new school were the front lines. Kong Le's troops, supplemented by Communist guerrillas, took up defensive positions in the second-floor classrooms. Across the street in the city cemetery, Phoumi moved his troops into place. Shooting from behind tombstones, they plastered the walls of the school with shot, trying to drive the Kong Le troops out. The following evening, Phoumi's troops were in the school, and Kong Le was trying to drive THEM out!

The White Army (Phoumi's soldiers wore a white scarf; Kong Le's men, a red one) was hiding in my school and in hurriedly dug trenches alongside. At dusk, from my vantage point in the rectory a few yards away, I saw Communist soldiers sneak along the far end of my property and slip into a small bamboo shed we had built for the construction workers. All was deadly quiet, for an hour. Then fierce fighting broke out. The Reds were firing 60mm. mortars, plus a heavy machine gun. At the start, Phoumi's soldiers didn't know exactly where the shells were coming from. They just shot back in the general direction. The next morning, the Communists were gone, and so was my bamboo hut! A heap of ashes remained.

December 14: I took my motorcycle and crept into town looking for something to eat. The Sisters who staffed the school, and I, had had little to eat for two days. Passing in front of the army headquarters, I saw that the once-beautiful buildings had been reduced to a heap of rubble. Kong Le, knowing that he could not defend the area, obliterated the entire block.

A few hundred yards past the headquarters I ran right into Phoumi's front-line troops. They advised me not to go farther, for they knew that a large number of Kong Le's snipers were hiding in shops and homes in that area. The "Whites" were creeping from hut to hut, shop to shop, trying to flush them out. I decided to leave my marketing for another day and turned around and went back to the relative safety of the rectory.

Most of Vientiane's civilian population had evacuated the city. In two days alone, ninety thousand people, out of a total population of one hundred thousand, had fled! One of the most heartbreaking sights took place one morning as I was helping to load a truck transporting Vietnamese and Lao refugees to Thailand.

There were sixty passengers, and Lord only knows how many blankets, bundles, and babies. The refugees wanted to take everything, naturally! Since the truck was so crowded, several of the male refugees started lightening the load by tossing overboard some of the bundles. The women went into hysterics. Many lost all their belongings, which had taken years of saving and sacrificing to accumulate. To quiet his wife, one man slapped her face. This only made her shout all the more. Fighting like wildcats, the women, with babies tightly held in their arms, fought the men to prevent them from throwing their belongings overboard — shouting and wailing all the time.

As Kong Le retreated northward to the hills, the city gradually calmed down and some semblance of normalcy was restored. On Christmas Day my church was dedicated.

Attended by a handful of priests and nuns and a few of the Lao Catholic men (their families still across the river in the haven of Thailand), the ceremony was brief and simple. In peacetime we would have had a much larger crowd, and a parish *boun,* to celebrate.

Nevertheless I was still very happy, and very proud. We were alive! The church still stood! — although a pockmark here and there betrayed the stormy world in which it stood.

As the Bishop pronounced the words transforming those walls of concrete block into a temple of God, I was grateful and proud. The procession wound its way around the outside of the church, weaving a path around the still-gaping mortar craters, reminders of the Free World's struggle against Communism. Reminders, too, of God's protection of his loved ones!

CHAPTER SEVENTEEN

Laura's Buggy

I BEGAN the year 1961 with mixed emotions. The church and rectory had been completed; the school still had another floor to go. The debris from the fighting — empty cartridge cases, shrapnel, the ashes of the bamboo hut — was shoveled out, and fresh cement plastered the pockmarks in the church and school walls.

What really counted now was the PEOPLE: activating and uniting them, making the parish something more than just a meeting place, making the people realize *they* were the Church.

The job wasn't going to be easy. Vientiane was still recovering from the shock of the five-month siege. Many of my Catholic families were homeless; some had lost a son, mother, father in the numerous battles. Food was scarce, prices sky-high, shops remained closed as merchants attempted to recoup their losses and begin again.

The diesel furnaces of the city electric plan were cleaned out and refired. Once again the city had its erratic public utility going. While ninety per cent of the city huts did not have electricity, nevertheless the feeble street bulbs on Lang Xang Avenue were a source of cheer and encouragement for all of us, signifying that life was getting back to normal.

A large section of the city had been burned to the ground. Each day my rectory was filled with refugees drifting back into the city, only to find their squalid huts a pile of ashes. Catholic Relief Services (CRS) shipped in tons and tons of food, clothing and medicine. With the Social Welfare department of the Lao Government, I had signed a formal contract launching our CRS program in Laos.

Feeding centers were set up in various sections of the city. There the refugees came in droves, seeking their rations of rice, powdered milk, and clothing. The border of Thailand and Laos was reopened, and trucks of CRS food poured across. We never knew at what hour of the day or night a truck would arrive, and we didn't care! To us, and to the refugees, the food-laden trucks were gifts from the gods!

Midnight would find me, assisted by one or two coolies, still unloading tons of powdered milk in the dim light of the truck's headlights. Lacking warehouse facilities, we seized any available space which provided shelter and protection against theft. The Fathers of *Le Sacré Coeur* rectory awoke one morning to find five tons of powdered milk stacked on their veranda. Classrooms at my new Notre Dame parish were converted into storage space and sorting rooms for the bales of clothing. Priests, nuns, catechists, parishioners, everyone, pitched in to move out the food and clothing as quickly as possible to the homeless and hungry. Seeing the Lao men and women of my parish enthusiastically hustling cartons of milk, heavy sacks of flour and rice, patiently wading through dusty bales of old clothes, I wondered why I was so concerned about "activating the laity" of my parish! Instinctively they banded together to help neighbors of theirs who were less fortunate than themselves.

* * *

During the Battle of Vientiane, all the cars belonging to the evacuated Americans were driven by USAID (U. S. Agency for International Development) to the U. S. Marine Base in Udorn, Thailand. Since Udorn was fifty miles from the Laos border, it was felt that the cars could be stored there safely until, and if, the owners ever returned from their refugee headquarters in Bangkok. Before it was possible to evacuate the cars to Thailand, however, some of them had been parked on the wartorn streets of Vientiane.

Early in 1961, as the Americans gradually returned to Vientiane, they would hustle over to Udorn to drive their cars back. The trip usually took the better part of a day. On arriving at the base, you would first have to find your car (somewhere among hundreds), then the keys to YOUR car. This could be quite a problem. Somewhere in the desk drawer of a Marine sergeant were your keys, as well as hundreds of sets of other keys, all shapes and sizes. Unlabeled, unidentified, this glorious conglomeration was deposited in the desk drawer and dragged out each time a weary American came to claim his wheels!

The battle of the keys completed, the next step was to get your car off the lot. Sounds simple? Try it! Especially after the car had been sitting for weeks in the broiling hot sun and thick dust.

Between Thailand and Laos there was the mighty Mekong to cross and, of course, no bridge! A slow-moving ferry grandly shuttled a maximum of six to eight vehicles across the river, the round trip taking anywhere from one to two hours, depending on how far downstream the current swept the ferryboat. Since there was a language barrier — or rather, a double language barrier, Thai and Lao — I accompanied several Americans to Udorn to help them bring their cars back to Laos.

One day a chic little American lady by the name of Laura Mayer asked me to accompany her to Udorn to claim her car. The bus trip to Udorn went well, taking only a couple of hours. We arrived at the base shortly before noon. Getting into the base was no problem, and, luckily, we spotted her little Dauphine within fifteen minutes after our search began. Then our problems started!

Obligingly the burly Marine sergeant pulled out his desk drawer and began fingering through the pile of keys. He found several that looked as if they would fit. They didn't. Then more looking, more perspiring, more keys. Occasionally a curt four-letter word would escape through his gritted teeth. "Sorry, Chaplain," he would mutter. Digging ever deeper into the drawer, he stirred the rusty pile of metal around.

Even the Marines have their limits! Slamming the drawer shut, he cut loose with several choice military phrases. "Don't worry, lady! I'll take care of you."

Out he went, striding determinedly toward the tiny Dauphine. Up went the hood. In went his head. As he tinkered with the ignition wires, the broiling Thai sun beat down on the back of the sergeant's already very red neck. But not a whimper from the dilapidated Dauphine.

He called over some of his buddies, and they pushed and pushed, and cursed and cursed. After fifteen minutes, all went into the mess hall for sandwiches and beer. Then, after they came out again, more pushing, more cursing.

Finally, with a sputter and a cough, the Dauphine battery came to life and we were off, much to the relief of a grease-splattered platoon of Marines!

As the Dauphine sputtered down the road, I turned its nose toward Nongkhai. When we passed through villages along the route, Thai farmers turned and stared at us. The tiny car looked as if it had been through the Battle of the Bulge. Machine gun holes ran zigzag up and down the sides, the windshield was long since gone, and the hot, dusty air blew into our faces. Every few miles we had to stop and fill the smoking radiator with water from the *klongs* (canals). The radiator, too, had been nicked by a bullet.

We nursed the car along, but it stopped dead within two blocks of Laura's home. Up went the hood for the "nth" time. "Thank God for those days in Wagner's garage," I thought as I lifted the hood. But nothing I could do would get the engine started again. Finally I found the trouble — at the other end! A bullet had nicked the gas tank and we had been dripping gas all afternoon!

Three years later, Laura was transferred to Seoul. Before she left, she made me a present of her Battle of Vientiane buggy.

FATHER MATT J. MENGER, O. M. I.

Exhausted refugees awaiting helicopter evacuation.

Gathering firewood to prepare the evening meal. The balance pole is indispensable to the Lao housewife.

Rats being sold in Vientiane's market.

Most countries have four wheels on their taxis...but not Laos!

Lao dancer in native dress performing traditional dance.

Just take a piece of bamboo, whittle a bit, and you have a pipe,...but not the coolest-smoking one in the world.

Sisters are the same all over the world—always working— here by the light of the kerosene lamp.

After seven years in Laos, it was back to Rome. The
warmly smiling priest is my Superior General, Very Rev.
Leo Deschatelets, O. M. I., one of the greatest heroes in
my life.

The baby, stuffed in a rice pot,
floated ashore near my rectory.
Another of the tragedies of life.

September, 1966. . . . The Mekong overflowed its banks, and
the streets of Vientiane became like this.

October, 1966.... Vientiane is bombed during a coup d'état led by General Ma. Repairing the damage at Our Lady of Hope Orphanage.

Fighting in the streets of Vientiane, this soldier paused for a soft drink while buildings around him blazed.

Boarding a plane and going off to visit the refugee camps.

An ordinary dirt road cut through the jungle serves as a runway. I took this photo from the rear door of a Caribou aircraft.

Typical mountaintop village in northern Laos.

Even Meo women become guerrilla fighters striving to keep
the mountains of Laos free.

Twelve-year-old boys in some parts of the world go to school and watch TV. But here in Laos....

A boy and his friend managed to escape from the Communists.

The years of suffering and sadness are forever etched in the lined face of this refugee woman.

These Meo refugee girls will have a glass of milk tonight, thanks to the generosity of the people of the United States and Catholic Relief Services.

A few bundles are all one can salvage out of a lifetime of work and sacrifice.

The young carry the young.

Agnes and her family arrive in Vientiane after their escape from a Communist-held village.

CHAPTER EIGHTEEN

The Glory of Paganism

OUR FACES WERE GRIMY, and our teeth gritty, from inhaling the red dust of the Paksane road. I was riding in the second car of our group, following Bishop Loosdregt, who was in the lead jeep with several other priests. We were en route to the Oblate minor seminary in Paksane for our annual retreat. After several hours on the dusty road, crossing rickety bridges, and sitting for hours in the broiling sun waiting for the slow-moving ferries, we were all exhausted and anxious to have the journey over with.

Six miles to go. Pulling up short, the lead car slowed to a stop. Ahead was a cluster of taxis and trucks. Climbing out of our jeeps, we walked over to a small group of people.

"*Men Nyang?* (What's up?)"

A taxi driver answered excitedly: "Pathet Lao laid land mines along this road last night. We cannot go on."

Joining the group, the Bishop overheard the driver's explanation. As he was pressed for more details, the taxi driver admitted that several trucks had passed through safely that very morning. Nevertheless, he was adamant. Land mines were somewhere in the road. He was sure of it!

"Wait here," Bishop Loosdregt said. "I'll lead off. If we get through, you follow behind. And if we don't...."

Holding my breath and whispering a Hail Mary, I watched the Bishop slide under the wheel of his car. Moving slowly, searching for the sight of tracks of the earlier trucks, he moved along in low gear. Ten yards... twenty... thirty... forty. The stretch of road was free of mines. We could move on.

As I switched on the ignition, my jeep crawled through the suspicious strip of road, hugging the tracks of the Bishop's wheels. Safely across, I waved to the people behind to come on through.

"Queing up" is the mode in Laos. One waits one's turn in line, calmly and patiently. Although the taxi driver we had spoken to had arrived at this spot after several other vehicles, he was angry at having lost precious hours on a wild rumor. Pulling ahead of the other cars, he shoved them out of the way so he could get through first, and thus make up the lost time.

Gathering speed, he set out. Less than twenty yards down the road, he swerved out of our tracks. "Voom!" The taxi flew into the air, the driver with it, as the wheels passed over the land mine! The rumor had been no rumor.

*　　*　　*

Two weeks of prayer, contemplation, reflection, and renewal of our vows. The period of the annual retreat passed quickly and uneventfully, with the exception of our unusual trip down and a black cobra which appeared sleeping peacefully in my bed one morning!

The dusty trip behind us, we returned to Vientiane once again. Unpacking the dirty laundry, I reflected on how good it was to be home again. I picked up my swimming trunks and clambered down the bank of the Mekong. A cool swim in the muddy river would be refreshing. After I spread my towel on the riverbank, I sat down and opened my breviary. I was looking forward to a few minutes of prayer while relaxing in the warm sun, then a refreshing swim.

My eyes squinted as a flicker of light raced across the page. Ignoring it, I continued reading. There it was again! Something was catching the rays of the sun. Looking up, I glanced at the water of the Mekong, softly lapping the shore. A rice pot lay on its side, washed ashore by the current. I walked over to it and bent down to pick it up and toss it back in the river.

As I lifted it and looked inside, I shuddered. The pot was not empty! A sodden cloth fell away, revealing the bloated body of a small infant. The repulsive odor of the decaying flesh reached my nostrils. Holding the pot gingerly, I set it down and examined the body.

The infant could not have been more than a few weeks old. It was well-formed, apparently healthy, judging from its weight and size. The only sign of imperfection was a harelip, that deformity so common here in Laos. Why had the baby been thrown into the river? Was it unwanted? Illegitimate? Had it been murdered? Or did it die a natural death?

I went back up the riverbank to the toolshed and got a shovel and some clean cloths. Then I returned to the quiet beach and dug a shallow grave. Wrapping the body in the cloths, I placed it in the grave, and filled in the excavated earth. I knelt, said the prayers for the deceased, and added a few prayers for the parents of this child.

As I picked up the shovel and my swim trunks and climbed the bank, my heart felt cold. No longer did the idea of a swim in the Mekong appeal to me.

Life in Laos is cheap — the cheapest commodity one can buy. I had experienced other incidents which proved it. In my rectory at Notre Dame one Sunday morning, I had overheard some Lao women discussing where one could buy a child. Picking up the infant son of a refugee woman sitting nearby, one old crone had dangled the baby by its heels. Calmly appraising it, she remarked, "I can get you four thousand kips (eight dollars) for this one!"

I was horrified, but not surprised. A human life can be bartered and sold much as one would barter and sell a scrawny chicken or a pig in the marketplace. This is paganism, in all its glory!

CHAPTER NINETEEN

White Gloves and Empty Hours

IN THE VERNACULAR OF THE STATE DEPARTMENT, the British Foreign Office, and other diplomatic bureaus, Laos is termed a "hardship post." In the vernacular of the bridge table, Laos is more aptly described as the place where "one goes up the walls!"

For the men of the foreign-service community, Laos is frustrating but fascinating, impossible yet intriguing. In the male animal, the instinct for adventure rises to the surface, mingled with the travel-bureau images of the exotic Orient. For the men, Laos offers the challenge of battle against Communism and the development of an undeveloped nation. For the women, it is something else.

Accustomed to escalators and elevators, shopping centers and drugstores, dreaming of theaters, discotheques, and boutiques, foreign-service wives struggle to keep their sense of humor and sanity. Vientiane, a capital city, is at the bottom of the list of potential four-star cities. Its few restaurants provide atmosphere with dim lights which serve more aptly to disguise the mysterious menu and the unpainted walls. The occasional movie at the local theater is endured to the smell of garlic and *padek* (a pungent pickled fish), and an occasional rat running over one's feet. Shopping forays mean plowing through the muck of the morning market to haggle price for something which one really doesn't want, and will probably leave behind when the tour is ended.

The first ride in the *sam loh* (three-wheeled bicycle taxi) is something which one must take in order to absorb local culture. The second ride occurs when the family car finds itself in the local garage for the "nth" time. The third ride is to be avoided at all costs!

Warned by public health officials of the danger of malaria and hepatitis, of unboiled water and unwashed vegetables, the diplomatic wife fills her days with unsuccessful attempts to learn the local language, with trips to the doctor for another of the endless series of inoculations, with boring hours on high heels attending yet another official dinner, tea, or reception, and of coping with her children, who quickly discard their shoes and go native.

Life exists in a state of suspension, in the euphoria of the recent R & R (Rest and Recuperation) in Bangkok or Hong Kong, where one devours pounds of iceberg lettuce and chewable beef, or in the expectation of mustering up the bucks needed for the next R & R.

For a missionary, life in a country such as Laos is no real problem. Sinking in his roots, he fills his days with three or four full-time jobs, studies languages, translates books into local dialects, ministers, treats, counsels, and hopes. At night the missionary is more than happy to click his beads and climb into bed.

But for the civilians of the Western world, life in Laos is a challenge — to keep one's sanity, to stick out the assignment, and to hope for a better post on the next tour. The question "Are you coming back?" often is met with either a groan of indescribable misery, or the elated grin of one who has served his time and is getting out!

Between *coups d'état,* the diplomatic community searches for something to occupy the long hours between breakfast and bed. The wife of one of the European diplomats arrived in Vientiane, excited and enthusiastic. Laos was a real challenge — one which would certainly give her husband's career a big boost up the ladder to an ambassadorial post. Grim and determined, despite the stories she had heard from other wives, she set to work to conquer Laos!

Armed with white gloves and calling cards, she sallied forth making the protocol-required official calls, dropping her cards at the multiple diplomatic residences. With that out of the way, she set to work unpacking her household freight. Duty called, a dinner was planned for the embassy staff; so she dug into the excelsior and sawdust. The best china, naturally, was on the bottom of the crate — in pieces. Her Austrian crystal was shattered. Some crates were quite simply missing. Her handmade lace tablecloth found itself twisted around the agitator as the native maid attempted to cope with that modern monster, the washing machine.

Undaunted, she gritted her teeth, and signed up for the various clubs — bridge group, women's club, volunteer hours in the local hospitals. Squinting her eyes, she stitched and sewed in the name of charity, and her husband's career.

She made peace with the snakes in her garden, and the servants who commandeered her kitchen. She dug in, resolutely averting her eyes when she confronted a calendar and the grim tidings that this tour still had another twenty months, three weeks, and six days to go!

The missing crates of ocean freight finally turned up, in another country, on another continent. Diverted, repacked, reshipped, they cleared the port and arrived on the doorstep of our disenchanted diplomatic wife. Unpacking her golf clubs, she sadly stored them away in the rear of the closet. Not at this post! When she asked her husband to buy her a TV set, she heard, for the thousandth time, "But, darling, this is Laos!"

Three other diplomatic ladies were in the same predicament. To sustain each other, they formed a bridge club. All afternoon, every afternoon, the ladies played bridge — and gossiped. After a week, our wife lost interest in bridge, and the gossip of the other three ladies.

"Ah, Jacques, *mon cher*," she greeted her husband excitedly one afternoon when he returned from the embassy, "guess what I'm going to do tomorrow morning. Jump out of an airplane!"

Before her startled husband could utter a word, she grabbed his arm, leading him upstairs. There in the middle of the bedroom was a large parachute. Slipping her arms through the straps, buckling them tight, she proudly stood in front of her husband.

"*Voilà!* Tomorrow morning Maurice is taking me for my first jump!" And she did it! Nearly two years later, when the embassy assigned her husband to another post, she was greatly bereaved when her husband would not permit her to take her parachute.

* * *

There are many ways to beat the system, and the boredom. Parachute-jumping is one of them. For the Lao citizens, social life is centered around the religious feast days and *bacis* signifying a marriage or the birth of a child.

In the villages, the people exist in a state of total isolation. There are no radios or newspapers. An exciting event in their lives occurs when the village is visited by the *mohlam,* a traveling singer or singing trio. *Mohlam* remains the most popular listening entertainment among the Lao and will gather more spectators than any other event in any village gathering.

An important feature of *mohlam* popularity is its ability to instruct and entertain at the same time. With lyrics improvised spontaneously, the singers ramble on about historical events. Quickly they switch to a point of religious doctrine and sing about it with wit and humor. The subject of love is rendered by sly jokes and with ingenious tones and sounds.

Those villages fortunately situated on the fringe of a city have become attracted to that miracle of the West, motion pictures. Villagers in the area of Vientiane walk many miles to see a movie. For the most part, the movies are American, Thai, Japanese, and Chinese. The sound track is usually Thai. Rather than use subtitles, the Lao remove the sound track and utilize "speakers." These usually have the same talents for interpretation and improvisation found in the *mohlam* singers. One speaker will furnish all sound for several parts in the movie, interpreting dialogue and story content in his own way. It is not uncommon for a male speaker to play both male and female roles, adapting his voice and personality to those of the movie characters.

One of the most famous speakers in Vientiane is a scrawny Lao named Souriya. Hustling through town in his rickety Land Rover, Souriya supplements his income from the movies by advertising events of local interest. The loudspeakers atop the truck blaring, Souriya drives through town promoting boxing matches, *bacis, bouns* — a roving "Madison Avenue" sputtering down the rue Circulaire.

For Christmas Eve at Notre Dame parish, I always organized a big *boun* and entertainment program. Starting about seven p. m., the program continued up to midnight Mass. While the program was entertaining, the real "gimmick" was to get the people to come to midnight Mass. Knowing that the Lao, once at home and in bed, would never "roll out" and walk through the pitch-black streets to church, I drew the parishioners to the *boun* and held them there until it was time for midnight Mass to begin.

The highlight of the *boun* each year was always the pageant depicting the story of Christmas. Atop a stage with scenery and backdrops made by the Lao parishioners, the play each year was produced and directed by the movie mogul — Souriya.

I remember one year in particular. The *boun* had been a tremendous success. Everyone was stuffed with *khao phoun,* a favorite Lao noodle made of rice flour. In the spirit of Christmas fun, someone had smuggled in some "lao-lao," the notorious Lao whisky. Something like "kick-apoo joy juice," lao-lao hits the stomach softly, and then explodes in a cascade of fire. One drink will hold the average man for several hours. Unfortunately, that evening, the director of the Christmas pageant had had more than one slug!

Paw Oat came on stage, draped in flowing robes he had borrowed. Swaying slightly, he began to narrate the story of Christ's birth. Then the production really hit its stride. On stage came Souriya. Playing several roles, he portrayed Joseph, Mary, and two shepherds. He put his incredible talent for mimickry to use by throwing in sound effects intended to take care of the donkeys, cows, and sheep.

Finally his script called for him to portray the angel who announced the great message to the shepherds. In a high falsetto "heavenly" voice, Souriya announced, rather thickly, that Christ had been born. As he listed slightly to one side, Souriya loudly proclaimed, "Peace on earth, to men of good will!" — and crashed to the floor. Another Christmas had come to Vientiane!

CHAPTER TWENTY

The Puppy Takes a Train

THE LIFE OF A MISSIONARY in a pagan land is one of ups and downs, peaks and lows, failures and successes. One of its lighter moments was related to me during a brief stay with the Redemptorist Fathers in Bangkok. Checking in at Holy Redeemer rectory, I cadged a few days of the Yankee hospitality for which the Redemptorists had become famous.

Over dinner one evening, Father Ray Brennan told me of his latest escapade. Accompanied by another young American priest, he had just arrived in Bangkok that morning, having traveled southward from Nongkhai aboard the daily train.

One of the Thai government officials in Nongkhai, a good friend of the missionaries, asked Father Ray to do him a favor. He wanted to send his puppy to Bangkok. Would Father Brennan mind taking care of the dog during the train trip?

"Of course not! It would be a pleasure!" Ray had replied. The official beamed his gratitude, agreeing to deliver the dog to the railway depot the next morning. Ray, in turn, would deliver the puppy to the man's family in Bangkok. No problem!

The next morning, Father Ray with his companion, Father Tony, was waiting in the depot. The train engineer was busily working up a full head of steam, and the conductor was making last-minute checks before pulling out. Up came the Thai official with his "puppy" — sixty pounds of German shepherd, three feet high, and with six inches of tongue! "This is the PUPPY?" Father Tony whispered to Father Ray out of the corner of his mouth.

Amid reassurances that they would take good care of the "puppy," the priests climbed aboard the train, the reluctant German shepherd trailing behind, straining on his leash. Heading into their compartment, the priests locked the door, sat down, and heaved a sigh of relief. Not much could happen to the dog aboard the train! They could relax until the next morning, when they would reach Bangkok. From the window they gave the traditional clasped-palm salute to the beaming Thai official as the train slowly pulled out of the station.

Clickety-clack, the train sped along its rails, destination Bangkok. Snugly installed in the small compartment, the sixty pounds of warm dog meat stretched across their feet, the priests recited their breviary and chatted as the miles fell away. Occasionally the dog would lift his ponderous head, his tongue sagging out of the corner of his mammoth jaw, and glance at one or the other of his "puppy sitters." Losing interest in his fellow passengers, the puppy would snuggle down more comfortably atop the priests' feet and drop off to sleep. Hours passed, the trip was going smoothly, and the train right on schedule.

When it pulled into Korat, the train slowed to a stop. Lowering the window to call one of the old ladies on the railway platform, Father Brennan began to haggle with her over the price of one of the roasted chickens which she was selling. Hanging out the half-lowered window, Father

Brennan busily jabbered away, gradually working the price down. Suddenly a blur shot past! Woosh! Out went the dog! After loping across the station platform, the German shepherd gained speed. "Come on, Tony!" Out the window leaped Father Brennan, Father Tony hard on his heels. As they raced down the side of the railroad tracks, the two priests chased the galloping German shepherd.

The whistle blasted! The train was ready to pull out! Turning on his heels, Father Tony raced back, shouting to the conductor: "Hold the train! Hold the train!"

Off in the distance, Father Brennan was gaining on the runaway shepherd. With a flying tackle, he grabbed trailing leash and errant dog, and the two of them rolled over in the dust. Picking himself up, wrapping the leash securely around his fist, Father Brennan dragged the unhappy puppy back to the train, leaping aboard as it rolled out of the station.

Under the baleful stare of the exasperated conductor, the two priests mustered their clerical decorum and grandly walked through the cars, led by a panting, slobbering German shepherd. When they reached their compartment door, they turned the handle. Nothing happened! "Try it again, Ray."

"Oh, oh, I just remembered. We locked the door from the inside so the dog couldn't get out!"

"Oh yeah!"

Turning on their heels, the dusty trio threaded its way through the various cars in search of the conductor.

"Pardon me, sir, but do you happen to have a key for Compartment 10-C?"

Staring at the bared teeth of the puppy, the conductor obligingly pulled out his roll of keys and headed for 10-C.

First key — no, that's not it. Second key, third, fourth. . . .
No luck. Not one fit. With a shake of his head and a
heavy sigh, the conductor turned and walked away.

As they squeezed into the narrow aisle in front of their
locked compartment door, the winded trio sat patiently on
the floor while the train rolled on. Passengers who came
through the aisle, awkwardly picked their way over the
sprawling legs of the two priests, and gingerly avoided
the slobbering jaws of the now exhausted puppy.

As the train pulled into Saraburi, the two priests went
outside. Under the open-mouthed stares of pedestrians and
passengers, Ray hoisted Tony up on his shoulder and
through the open window of Compartment 10-C.

Once again within the privacy of their compartment,
one rambunctious puppy was tied to the door handle, the
window securely bolted, and the shade firmly pulled down
in the faces of the curious onlookers!

CHAPTER TWENTY-ONE

Around the World on Five Bucks

THE BISHOP INSISTED. I refused. This had been going on for fully fifteen minutes. Finally, the kindly Bishop eased back in his chair, looked over his cluttered desk at me, and said: *"Très bien, mon père.* I don't know how you will be able to do it, but still I admit I would be very grateful if you could. We do need the money very badly."

He didn't have to finish. There had been the same obstacle ever since my arrival in Laos, five years previously. Lack of money! And I was determined not to use any of the vicariate's precious dollars for a plane ticket home.

My home leave had been set for 1962, and the Bishop and I were arguing over my "mode of travel." Knowing how hard-pressed he was for money, I had requested permission to thumb my way home. Envisioning one of his missionaries stranded somewhere between Laos and the shores of the States, the Bishop at first rejected my suggestion. After each new argument, the saintly Bishop would nod his head and smile, "I know, but...."

After much discussion, I won. The Bishop gave me permission to thumb my way over 25,000 miles of land and sea, and I agreed to take his five dollars just in case I got stranded.

The last few weeks before my departure were hectic. Saying farewell to the parishioners of my newly built

AROUND THE WORLD ON FIVE BUCKS 139

Notre Dame, I gathered messages and addresses of people to contact in the U. S., and I attended many *bacis*. During a bon-voyage dinner hosted by the Honorable Ky-Quan-Thanh, Vietnamese Ambassador to Laos, I was asked what airline I was taking. "Any one that takes me!" I answered.

After I had explained my daring proposal a little more thoroughly, the Ambassador said: "Father, my Beechcraft has to go down to Saigon this week. What day would you like to go?" Three days later, the Bishop's five bucks in my pocket, I was aboard the Vietnamese Embassy's plane en route to Saigon, and the U. S.

Strolling down the rue Catinat in Saigon, I saw a sign reading "Fly Cathay Pacific." "O. K., I will!" I said to myself, and into the airline office I strode. The pert little receptionist seemed very baffled, to say the least, when I asked if I could thumb a ride on her next plane to Hong Kong. With a lifted eyebrow, she politely led me into the manager's office.

Cathay Pacific deserves a gold star! After listening to my "dare" (to go round the world on five dollars), the manager said: "Why just to Hong Kong? We don't fly to the States, but we do go as far as Tokyo." Buzzing for the petite receptionist, he told her, "Write Father Menger a ticket for Tokyo on our next flight."

Stopping over in Hong Kong, I headed for the Catholic Relief Services office. With Msgr. John Romaniello, director of the CRS Hong Kong program, I spent two days visiting refugee resettlement sites and social centers.

When I dropped in to see my good friend Captain Harry Patterson, I chalked up another gold star. This one for States Marine Line, of which Harry was the Asian bureau chief. As he handed me the shipping schedule,

Harry said: "Father, take your pick of boat, port, and date. You have a bunk on any of our ships, provided you don't mind freighters."

I chose Yokohama as the port, and January 1, 1962, as the time of my final embarking for the U. S. On our first afternoon out, a nasty tropical storm blew up. High winds whipped up waves that came hurtling over the bow. This lasted for two days. I admired our crew. They kept our bobbing freighter upright on course. Unfortunately I couldn't say the same for my stomach!

I was met at the Oakland pier by a group of army officers and their wives whom I had known in Vientiane. Colonel and Mrs. Sanders insisted that I drive down to their home in Carmel to spend a few days with them. Accepting gratefully, I headed for Carmel. Not only had I known the Sanders in Laos, but Bridget Sanders and I had grown up together in San Antonio. Classmates at St. Martin's Hall, we reminisced about the "good old days" while Bridget stuffed me with good American food.

I was back in the U. S.! Everything seemed, and WAS, so very different from the little Kingdom of Laos I had left behind. It was a novelty to see signs and billboards in English; the bright neon lights seemed brighter than they had five years before. We toured I. Magnin's at Carmel, where Bridget held down her position as manager. Walking around the streets, I found the grocery stores in California a gourmet's delight. Back in their home, Bridget smilingly remarked: "Look! No filters, no boiling of water! Just turn on the tap and drink!" I hadn't been able to do that in five years.

The States had everything! Why would any American complain? During my weeks and months in the U. S., however, I learned that some Americans did complain and protest about many, many things. Each time I was irked, and angry! I wanted to shout from the housetops: "Be grateful to your country, and your God! The guy on the other side of the world hasn't got it so good!"

With a foot-long list of speaking engagements spread over the coming ten months, I set out from California, my five dollars still intact. Climbing into a sleek Ford donated by a sympathetic used-car dealer, I set off for the tour. Up the Blue Ridge Mountains, over the Skyline Drive, in and out of New York, Pennsylvania, Washington, Louisiana, Texas, Kentucky, I crisscrossed the country. Logging countless thousands of miles in the Ford, speaking to anyone and everyone who would listen, I told the story of Laos.

As I sat in the office of Senator Thomas Dodd, we discussed the explosive situation in Laos, Vietnam, and other parts of Southeast Asia. "Father Menger, the other Senators should hear this," he said. "Would you have time to address a group of them?" Buzzing for his secretary, Senator Dodd gave instructions and, a few days later, I found myself at the head of a long conference table in a mammoth room. "Senate Foreign Relations Sub-Committee," read the bronze plaque on the door.

It was an extremely friendly and lively exchange. For an hour and a half I answered the patient questions and probing of the Senators. Seeing their keen interest, I was fully aware that these men, just a small number out of the two hundred million Americans, were really the shapers of U. S. policy to Laos and to Asia. Their questions, which were many, showed it. After our meeting, Senator Dodd and I taped several radio interviews to be broadcast later in the week.

A few weeks later I was in Houston. Answering the telephone, I heard: "Father Menger? Could you come to Washington to lecture at the Military Attaché School?" It was the school's executive officer on the telephone.

Again I accepted, and again I found a group of our country's leaders truly interested and concerned with Southeast Asia. As I stood at the rostrum in the packed, multi-tiered auditorium, I quickly estimated the audience as between 150 and 200. All were field-grade officers; they were destined to be scattered throughout the world, wherever our United States maintained an embassy. How much would the future of the United States depend on the reports and judgments of these men? Very, very much!

Again I encouraged the men to ask questions. And they did. I'll never forget one hand I saw raised way in the back of the auditorium, high up in one of the last tiers. "Colonel, what is your problem?" I called to him.

A tall husky officer with an eagle in his lapel, rose to his feet. I later learned that he had been quite a hero in the Korean War. "Father Menger," he began. There was a brief silence. I could tell he was a bit hesitant to go on. Finally he did. "What do the people of Laos REALLY want?"

I had not expected that question. All of the previous discussion had been confined to the military, political, economic, even geographic aspects of Laos.

"Colonel, the people of Laos want the same thing you and I want."

"What's that?"

"Happiness!"

Leaving behind the world of politics and diplomacy, I bade farewell to the capital's "Foggy Bottom" and turned the nose of the Ford toward St. Paul. I checked in at the Oblate provincial house and tackled my lengthy list of speaking engagements. For the next four weeks, driving along the frozen highways of Minnesota, I pleaded, prayed, and begged for Laos.

During my stay at 15 Montcalm Court, I had been shuttling around the nearby cities and towns. Since I came and went at odd hours, the Fathers had finally mustered up a door key for me. On one trip, however, I had accidentally left it behind. Finding the key in my room, Father Aloysius (Al) Svobodny and Father Boniface (Boni) Wittenbrink waited up each night in case I would return. After the third day — and still no Menger — Al and Boni gave up, not knowing whether I would return that night or not.

Not wishing me to be obliged to sleep on the front lawn, they sought a way of putting the house key outside. But how to tell me where it was hidden, without, of course, telling any burglar who happened to pass by? Al and Boni solved the problem in typical sacerdotal fashion. Hiding the key outside, they taped a note to the door and went to bed.

Two a. m. I pulled up to the provincial house. I stared up at the darkened windows and wondered whom I would have to arouse. When I reached the door, I glimpsed a piece of white paper fluttering in the breeze. Striking a match, I read the brief epistle telling me — in LATIN! — "The key is under the mat!"

No country in the world has as many generous hearts and sympathetic souls as the United States. Struggling to understand the mysterious world from which I had come, they recognized the suffering of their brothers and sacrificed for them. Two hundred TV and radio shows and three hundred lectures later, I made plans for my return to Laos. The Bishop's five dollars in my wallet, still unspent, nestled alongside a return-trip airline ticket, the gift of a family in Washington, D. C.

Saying good-bye to Dad and my relatives in Texas, I flew to Kentucky, and the Abbey of Gethsemani. My last thirty days in the States were spent at the Trappist Abbey, where I made a retreat and the second novitiate required by the Oblate Rule. Inspired by the nearness and sanctity of Father Louis (Thomas Merton), Father M. Raymond, and the other saintly monks, I renewed my vows, and my determination, to bring the God of Gethsemani to the pagans of Laos.

CHAPTER TWENTY-TWO

The Blood I Saw Was Real

As THE AIR LAOS DC-3 banked over the muddy Mekong on its final approach into Wattay airport, I fastened my seatbelt, thinking, "Home, at last!" I was returning to Laos encouraged by the interest of the people back in the U. S., and convinced that the future of Asia would determine the future of America.

Peering through the dirty window of the plane, I could see the dusty streets of Vientiane, the arid rice fields surrounding the airport, the bamboo huts listing on their stilts. Nothing had changed! Poverty, misery, and suffering still reigned supreme in Laos.

But newscasts and wire service reports of the past months told a different story. The Geneva Agreement signed in July, 1962, guaranteed the neutrality and independence of my tiny kingdom. Moreover, it supposedly guaranteed the freedom of the people of Laos from the harassment, torture, and attempted domination of its Communist citizens and their Red neighbors to the north!

Politically the situation in Laos was explosive. Thus I was not surprised at the obviously tense atmosphere at Notre Dame rectory when I checked in that afternoon. Colonel Ketsana, former Chief of Staff for Kong Le, and No. 2 man in the Neutralist army, had been assassinated in his home near Xieng Khouang. Khamphery, a director of the Ministry of Education, had been cut down by assassin's bullets. On April 1, Quinim Pholsena, Secretary of Foreign Affairs, was ambushed as he was getting out of his car. Returning from a palace reception hosted by the King of Laos, Quinim and his wife were shot by one of his own guards, a corporal. Madame Quinim survived with slight injuries. Her husband died instantly.

The Troika Government established by the Geneva Agreement provided for a coalition government of Royalists, Neutralists, and Communists. The Troika never got off the ground. Enraged by the assassination of Quinim (reportedly because of his pro-Communist attitude), the Pathet Lao Communist troops attacked the Neutralist forces in Xieng Khouang province. Fighting broke out throughout the entire area. My skeptical opinion of the feasibility of a Troika Government was confirmed by General Phoumi Nosavan, leader of the Royalist forces.

Encountering the General at a diplomatic reception, I asked his opinion of the situation in Laos. He was very frank.

"Many people think our coalition government is advancing, Father," he said. "We are moving forward all right, but we are not getting any closer together." An ironic smile on his face, he sipped his drink, continuing: "A coalition government in Laos? You can compare it to two railroad tracks. Instead of going parallel, we are getting even more and more distant from each other."

I was forced to agree with him. A coalition government of such divergent factions could never work. Imagine, if you will, the United States ruled and directed jointly by Richard Nixon, Mao Tse-tung, and Indira Gandhi! — or Eldridge Cleaver, George Wallace, and Benjamin Spock!

The ground rules for the Laos coalition government required all three rulers to agree before any law could be effected. In 1963 I returned to a very bleak and pessimistic country.

Economically the country was stagnating. Totally dependent on imports and foreign aid, forced to maintain an army and conduct a war which devoured manpower and local resources, the people of Laos moved further backward in time.

Neutralists sidetracked, Royalists retreated, and the Communists advanced, pushing through Sam Neua and Xieng Khouang provinces, turning the green-velvet Plain of Jars into a bloody red carpet. We missionaries held our breath, and prayed, as Laos faced her greatest trial in modern history. As the people of Laos suffered, so, too, did the Church.

Étienne Loosdregt, French by birth, is one of the most unassuming men in the history of the Church. Gentle, serene, and unflappable, he had labored for thirty-six years in this pagan kingdom. Already twice a prisoner of war — first of the Vietnamese, then, during World War II, of the Japanese — operating on one lung, having lost the other to tuberculosis in the early years of his ministry, he led his men and flock with a quiet courage and steely determination.

Despite the urgings of his priests, the Vicar Apostolic of Vientiane boarded an International Control Commission plane and flew to Xieng Khouang city. Concerned about the safety of his priests and nuns, the Bishop felt that his presence would encourage them to hold out as long as possible.

Two days after his arrival, Communist troops broke through the fragile lines of the Royalist forces and occupied the province of Xieng Khouang. The Bishop and all the inhabitants of the school, orphanage, convent, and rectory were placed under house arrest.

For several weeks, 105mm. shells rained down around the mission. In one night bombardment, several mortar shells hit the orphanage; five children were killed and twelve injured. Shortly afterwards, the church was partially destroyed by more shelling. The following day the Communist soldiers apologized, but still the bombardments and shelling continued.

In Vientiane, the International Control Commission attempted to negotiate with the Communist forces through the Troika Government. Their pleas for the release of the missionaries and children were ignored. World opinion was aroused as news of the capture of the Vicar Apostolic of Vientiane hit the wire services around the globe.

Through private channels the French and British embassies submitted formal requests to the Communists to release their captives and permit their safe passage out of the war zone. Silence! Meanwhile, wounded civilians and neutralist soldiers, brought to the Catholic Mission in Xieng Khouang, were treated by the missionaries. Loudspeakers from Communist outposts blared out that the missionaries were "traitors to the cause, because they are collaborating with the enemy!"

The presence of the Bishop became a thorn in the side of his Communist captors. Criticized in the world press for their detention of innocent children and nuns, put on the spot by the Bishop, who adamantly refused to leave unless the nuns, priests and children could accompany him, the Communists came face to face with the ironclad determination of Étienne Loosdregt.

After forty-six days of house arrest, the Bishop, ten priests and nuns, plus fifty orphaned children, were placed aboard planes of the International Control Commission and guaranteed a safe passage to Vientiane by the Communist leaders.

* * *

Sam Tong is a tiny village seventy-five miles north of Vientiane, perched on the plateau of a high mountain. This was one of the major refugee centers because of its strategic location. Aboard an Air America helio in September, 1963, I headed north to check on distribution of Catholic Relief Services food to refugees.

Coming into Sam Tong is something like being a fly buzzing around and down inside a teacup. Looking out the windows of the single-engined craft as it contentedly hummed along, I could see the towering, jagged crests so characteristic of northern Laos.

Ray Salucci, the pilot, gave me the "thumbs-down" signal, indicating that we were coming in for a landing. I could see nothing but mountains in all directions. Carefully skirting the top of a five-thousand-foot peak, Ray banked to the left, swung the aircraft through a crack in the mountains, and nosed down, circling slowly to lose altitude. Sam Tong airstrip lay directly below.

Laos from the air is magnificent! The mountains are incredibly beautiful — rough, rugged, jagged peaks that seem to scratch the sky. The foliage is thick, dense, lush green, with trees and plants covering the mountains from base to peak. Guarded by these giants are rich valleys which from the air seem to be paradise. Living in them, however, is something unlike living in the Garden of Eden!

Waiting for Ray to refuel, I trotted down the trail to the hospital which had been built by USAID. Edgar ("Pop") Buell, the American representative of USAID at Sam Tong, accompanied me. The hospital consisted of two frame buildings, each housing a thirty-bed ward. The beds were planks slightly elevated above the dirt floor, and the bedding nothing more than a thin blanket. It was cold. The temperature was between forty and forty-five degrees, and the wind cut through my jacket. I shivered at the sight of scrawny patients wrapped in their thin blankets and huddled on their planks trying to keep warm.

Even these primitive buildings were at that time a major accomplishment. Carving Sam Tong out of a jungle, USAID had to fly in everything — planks, tin, medicines.

According to pronouncements from the Western world, the war in Laos was limited to minor skirmishes. But minor or not, the blood I saw was real. There was the nineteen-year-old boy who had stepped on a land mine. He had been a soldier since he was fifteen, and all he wanted was to go back home to Savannakhet. I saw another boy with part of his face shot away and a bloody bandage over his eye. I saw the blood, the look in the eyes of wounded, frightened soldiers. In the distance came the popping noises of M-1's and carbines as Communist and Neutralist patrols met each other in the mountains. I felt that knot in my stomach that comes when war is no longer something you read about in newspapers.

Swinging aboard the refueled helio, Ray and I took off for Ban Na, a fifteen-minute hop farther north. The people of Ban Na were my first parishioners back in 1957, when I had been assigned to the village of Khang Si. After they had been driven out by advancing Communist forces, they had resettled in Ban Na.

Buzzing the Ban Na airstrip, which ran uphill, ending at the base of a mountain, we chased the horses and pigs off the runway and banked to make our final approach. As Ray kept the motor running, I hopped down and ducked out of the prop wash. Winding down the side of the mountain was a footpath. A third of a mile down, the village perched on the side of the mountain. As I picked my way along the path around the pigs, I was accompanied by a crowd of inquisitive Meo natives who lived atop the mountain near the airstrip.

All of Ban Na turned out to welcome Khoun Pha home. I hadn't seen them in seven years, but it could have been only seven days to them. Everyone in the village was Catholic, and the faith of the people was tremendous. Nightly they met in the chapel to recite the rosary.

We went into the church. It was nothing more than a bamboo hut hanging precariously on the side of the hill. The floor was strips of woven bamboo. The altar was an old ammo case covered with a parachute. There was no tabernacle, only a crudely carved crucifix, and the presence of a simple, basic, enduring faith.

I gave a short homily, and asked whether anyone wanted to go to confession before Mass. Hundreds of hands went up. Knowing that I had only two hours in the village, I bestowed general absolution on the congregation and began Mass.

After the short service I was invited to the mayor's hut for lunch. In my honor the family had killed one of their few chickens. The house was about two hundred square feet in area and was divided into two sleeping cubicles and one main room. Two wood fires blazed. As the smoke bit into my eyes, I was kept busy wiping away the tears. Crowded into the hut were the village leaders, half a dozen women busily preparing the meal and, at the door, all the children of the village. We drank rice wine out of bamboo straws three feet long and squatted on stools as the women served the chicken stew and rice.

It was with regret that I bade farewell to Ban Na. I knew that it would be many months before the people would have Mass again. I began the steep climb to the top of the mountain. I had agreed with Ray to be at the airstrip no later than two-thirty p. m. Climbing aboard the helio, we headed this time for Muong Cha, a new refugee camp just being established. For the past fifteen days a group of five hundred refugees had been walking out of Communist-held territory. Carrying their old people and sick, the refugees had been kept alive by airdrops of food. The camp was hurriedly erected in the valley, and food, shelter, and medicines were being readied for the occupants. Camouflage parachutes had been hastily set up to provide shelter. Army tents served as dispensary, quarantine ward, surgery. Guarding the camp was a battalion of Lao army troops.

The Muong Cha refugee camp sat in a miniature valley, guarded on three sides by towering mountains and, on the fourth, by limestone cliffs. As I toured the camp with the commanding Colonel, a C-47 began a circling pass over the valley. The double door on the side of the plane had been removed. We could see the two "kickers" standing in the doorway.

Seeing that the drop zone was clear, the pilot banked and came in for a second pass. On signal from the cockpit, the two kickers in the rear of the plane gave a shove to the pallets of rice and bulgur wheat. Out the door they sailed, thudding and echoing throughout the valley as they landed. One of the Americans standing nearby mused, "You know we've got a whole generation of kids in Laos who think rice comes from airplanes!"

How true, I thought! Thousands of children in Laos have never known any life beyond that of the refugee camps. Their families displaced, they have never had "roots" — a hut, a village, a rice field the family could farm. Life from the moment of birth has been nomadic, a matter of fleeing from one camp to another, from one jungle to another, from one mountain to another. These people had been kept alive by the planes that circled low, dropping pallets strapped with sacks of food. Yes, I'm quite sure a few of those children thought that rice grows in airplanes!

The men who fly these planes have extraordinary courage. Hitting the drop zone at an altitude of eight hundred to one thousand feet calls for pinpoint skill and precision. In strategic areas the planes are "sitting ducks" for ground fire from guerrillas. The pilots and their kickers, ignoring the danger, have kept thousands of refugees alive, dropping their sacks on tops and flanks of mountains, and in the pinhead-sized drop zone buried in the thickness of the jungle.

In Laos the airdrop has developed into a science. Experimenting with various-size containers and pallets, the USAID team has refined the process to such a degree that the loss factor is less than ten per cent on free-fall drops.

The eighty-pound sacks of rice are lashed with special knots and heavy duty ropes to plywood pallets and then loaded aboard the aircraft.

Over the drop zone, the pilot hits the buzzer. In the aft cabin, the kickers put their feet to the pallets and shove. Out the door sail the pallets, the sacks breaking loose and landing scattered precisely over the drop zone.

Two of my close friends were kickers on the airdrop planes. Joe and Ed were sharing a room in my rectory. Each morning, Joe would be up at five a. m. to serve my Mass before departing on the day's missions.

One day the boys were working aboard a Caribou, a plane used frequently for airdrops. For some unexplainable reason, Ed was not wearing his parachute. As the signal flashed red, indicating that the aircraft was over the drop zone, Joe and Ed shoved at the sacks, pushing them down the ball-bearing skids and out the rear of the plane. Losing his balance, Ed slid down with the pallets. As he was going out the door, he grabbed the metal rim of the door frame. Joe attempted to grab Ed by the hair. His fingers slid through the boy's crewcut, and Ed fell to his death.

When the plane landed, Joe was in a state of shock. Put under sedation immediately, he was evacuated to a field hospital in Thailand. That night, as the plane was being readied for its regular flight the next morning, the maintenance crew noticed in the doorway splatters of blood and pieces of teeth.

The shock grounded Joe for several months, but he came back to Laos, and resumed his job as kicker, feeding the hungry refugee kids who think that rice comes out of the sky!

CHAPTER TWENTY-THREE

In the Opium Den

THE MORNING OF MY THIRTY-SIXTH BIRTHDAY I finished Mass, doffed the silk vestments and white cassock, and donned a pair of faded blue dungarees.

My parish of Notre Dame had been turned over to Père Jean-Paul Brouillette. The Bishop had assigned me to take charge of several construction projects. When they were completed, I was to direct the new Vientiane orphanage, Our Lady of Hope.

Spring arrived in Laos and the balmy pre-monsoon months passed in a flurry of activity. My first construction job was the building of a chancery office and residence for the Bishop. Everything went smoothly. The main building completed, I moved in my books and clothes as we put on the finishing touches in preparation for the arrival of Bishop Loosdregt and the other priests. But they couldn't move into the *Évêché*, nor could I remain, unless we had water.

The municipal water system was confined to the central part of Vientiane, an area of less than ten square blocks. Two miles down the road from the site of the new *Évêché* was the last meter of pipe carrying city water. Thus, if we wanted water, we would have to dig our own well.

That sounds relatively simple. You dig a hole, keep going down until you break through laterite, sand, gravel, and hit water. No water, keep digging. No one can tell where the water is. It might be twenty feet or one hundred feet from the top. Once you hit water, you sink concrete cylinders to hold the sides of the well and prevent cave-ins. Add a little cement to bind the framework together, hook up your pump, and you have water!

Never having dug a well before, I left this job till the last, completing the twenty-room *Évêché* first. Finally I assigned a crew of coolies to start digging. Chop and Sieng were in the first brigade. When they had dug down twenty feet, they broke through laterite and started hitting sand and gravel. Great! This was a good indication that water was not too far away. We wouldn't have to dig too deeply.

Gas fumes began to filter into the well. Having to work the crew in shifts, never permitting one man to be down the well more than ten minutes, I added another crew, this time led by Dat, a Vietnamese refugee who was my carpentry foreman. As the coolies dug ever deeper, the gas fumes increased. Down in the hole, a shout would bring all of us running as the walls of the well cracked, showering the coolie in the pit with suffocating mud.

We were getting no closer to water, and the danger was increasing daily. Finally both crews refused to go down into the well. What to do? Without water, the *Évêché* was a beautiful structure sitting majestically on the banks of the Mekong, but uninhabitable!

"*Khoun Pha,* the only ones who will go down into that well are the opium smokers," Chop told me. With a desperate need for money to sustain their habit, the opium smokers took on the most dangerous jobs, work that no one else would do for any amount of money. Thus I boarded my Honda and went into town to the local opium den, searching for a team of well-diggers.

The den was situated on one of the back alleys of the city. I had been there several times before, summoned by members of a family to minister to their dying brother, father, or husband.

Turning right at the morning market, I steered the Honda down Sam Sen Thai Street and headed for the Nong Boua sector of town. Then, as I made my way into a narrow path, I slowed the Honda. The path tapered off into a narrow trail. After parking and locking the motorcycle, I continued on foot.

Ahead was a small tin shed. Rusty and dilapidated, it sagged on one end. The wooden door was encased in a tin framework and attached with rusty hinges. As I walked up to the door, I hesitated for a moment. I gave two short raps and paused. Then one loud rap. A pause. Finally three rapid light taps. This was the signal to the inhabitants of the den that the caller was a friend. When the door slowly creaked open, I stepped over the threshold. A shriveled old lady quickly closed and bolted shut the door.

"*Paw Oat le Paw Tao u ni bo?*" I asked.

"*Doy, Khoun Pha.*" With a slight gesture, she indicated a corner of the opium den where I could find the two men for whom I was searching.

I stood for a moment, waiting for my eyes to adjust to the dim light. For a few seconds, all I could see was blurred splotches of flickering lights on the dirt floor. Then, as my eyes began to get accustomed to the darkness, I could make out rough planks, nailed together, elevated a foot off the floor. All the beds were filled. About half of them had tiny flickering lamps on the edge next to the occupant's head. The occupants were in the process of smoking their opium.

The room was filled with an overpowering, sweet aroma, gagging in its thick, musky fragrance. Dipping an eight-inch metal pick into the tin containers of crude opium, the smokers would extend it over the flame, continuously revolving the pick. When the opium had attained the required temperature, they dropped it into their opium pipes. Taking several deep, rapid, long draws on the pipe, the smokers would lie back, swooning into nirvana for several hours.

The twenty-bed den was always full. Many were permanent boarders. Paw Oat and Paw Tao were itinerant unskilled workers. Thus they had little ready cash to sustain a regular daily habit of opium. Whenever they would be lucky enough to hold a job for a few days, they would collect their salary and scurry to the opium den.

Many women and children — families of the men on the beds — were crowded into the stifling room. They had brought some rice and other food to their husband's or father's "bed." The women would coax their men to eat just a little. When the smoker would return to his narcotic heaven, the women would quietly pick up their suppers of uneaten food and return to their poor huts. The addiction of the men condemned their wives, children, and families to a life of abject poverty.

I found Paw Oat and Paw Tao on two beds in a corner of the room. Their eyes were bloodshot, and they reeked of the foul air of the den. Having run out of kips, they were preparing to check out and vacate their beds for other hopeless victims of the poppy.

The two men gathered up their few belongings and followed me outside. Blinking in the bright sunlight, they listened as I offered them the job of digging my well. After a few minutes of haggling, they agreed. Their only stipulation: I was to pay them each day! When I looked into their gaunt faces and bloodshot eyes, I saw through their ruse. After collecting their pay each night, they would head for the opium den, light up, and drift through a narcotic haze for the next twenty-four hours. That meant my well would get dug every other day. Nothing doing!

"Tell you what I'll do, Paw Oat," I said. "When you finish digging the well, I'll give you your salary for every day the job takes, plus a bonus of a thousand kips (two dollars)." His eyes lit up at the thought of an extra two bucks' worth of opium. Quickly he and his crony agreed.

The next morning the two addicts reported for duty. Stripping to their loincloths, they listened as I carefully explained what they must do. Paw Oat slid down the rope to the bottom of the well. On top, Paw Tao was responsible for keeping a sharp watch for signs that gas fumes were threatening to overcome Paw Oat. To do this, the guy on top had to keep up a running conversation with the guy on the bottom. Slow responses, lags in the conversation, were signs that the fumes were beginning to overpower the coolie in the pit. Quickly he would be hauled up for some oxygen, and rest.

Everything went smoothly for a few hours. On the bottom of the well, Paw Oat shoveled mud and water into the bucket and signaled Paw Tao to haul it up. I turned my attention to the painters and carpenters within the house, giving them directions as they completed the interior of the *Évêché*.

"*Ravang de! Ravang de!*" Muffled and far away, the words floated to the surface. I hustled over to the well and bent down.

"*Men nyang?*" I called down the gaping hole.

From forty feet below came the frail voice, "*Kou tok hua!*" Turning to the poor opium addict at my side, I asked Paw Tao what he had done. His attention distracted, no doubt dreaming of another visit to the local den, he had sent a bucket down the pulley too fast, clunking Paw Oat on the head. A stream of Lao curse words came singing up the gaping hole, followed by the rope carrying a bloody Paw Oat.

* * *

Despite a gashed head and a careless partner, Paw Oat completed the digging of the well. The Bishop moved into his new home, and I turned my attention to clearing fifteen acres of brush and jungle for the new orphanage, Our Lady of Hope. The Sisters had arrived from Savannakhet to open the orphanage, the orphans were jammed into temporary quarters at Dong Palan, and everybody was standing by, impatiently waiting for Menger to get on with the job! After paying off my opium smokers and transferring the construction crew to the new building site at Kilometer 8, I grabbed my faithful helper Nouchin and headed for the new property.

It was a beautiful tract of land. Unfortunately, though, no one could see its beauty but me! The day I took the Bishop and the other Fathers out for a look, we stood at the edge of the property and stared into thick thorn bushes and termite hills two feet ahead. It was literally impossible to see through the brush. "Isn't it beautiful?" I would ask. A very skeptical, *"Ah oui, mon père,"* would invariably come from the visitor as he craned his neck, looking up the eight- and ten-feet high termite hills.

Pulling out his machete, Nouchin began to slash his way through the brush, with me at his side. We had to mark out the property line to put up our fence. That job done, we could get to work clearing the terrain. After several hours of hacking, we sat down for a breather. Both of us were totally disoriented. With only the sun to keep us going vaguely in the right direction, I knew it would be an impossible job to site landmarks and mark off correctly the boundaries of our property. Finally, I hit upon an idea!

With my two hands on his rear, I gave Nouchin a shove and sent him shinnying up a three-story-high *mai khaeng* tree. We were in the thickest brush of the fifteen acres, the most difficult side of our property line, and the most important to stake off. With Sieng and Chop wielding the machetes, Nouchin perched in the tree with the scrap of paper denoting our title to the land. We set out.

"Leo sci! Leo sci!" he would yell. Turning to the left, we would slash a few more feet. *"Leo kwa! Leo kwa!"* Hearing Nouchin's yell to turn right, we would hack a few more feet in that direction. *"Pai thang nya* (Go straight ahead)" — the coolies and I pushed on. Coming face to face with a termite hill, dragging our marking twine behind us, we would climb up, over, and down the other side, the marking twine following us. After a hot afternoon in the brush, we succeeded in marking the fourth, and last, side of our property. Breathing a sigh of relief,

we headed back to the *mai khaeng* tree to collect Nouchin and head for home.

Suddenly an indignant trumpeting stopped us in our tracks. An elephant! The full-grown beast was the pet of General Khouprasith, commandant of the nearby Chinaimo army camp. Each morning a private would lead the beast down the road and into the brush to forage during the day. Unfortunately the elephant's choicest nibbles were on the property of Our Lady of Hope.

No animal is more feared in Laos than the elephant. And this particular pet had a reputation for knocking down fences and charging anyone who got in his way. Lifting his trunk, he sniffed the air. Smelling Nouchin, who was perched precariously atop the *mai khaeng* tree, the elephant was becoming more and more angry by the minute. His private hunting preserve had been invaded!

We yelled to Nouchin to "sit tight," and moved downwind to a safer area. Every time the elephant nudged the tree, a feeble and frightened "oooh" would drift out from the branches. Nouchin, hanging on for dear life, endured a terrifying fifteen minutes as the elephant spent his anger hammering the tree with his trunk and roaring threats.

Bored with his elusive quarry and hungry for bamboo shoots, the elephant lumbered away. Nouchin scampered down the tree and set an all-time cross-country record heading for the Land Rover!

With the property lines marked off, work got underway in clearing the tract of land for construction of the orphanage building. It was a particularly tense year. We had had one *coup d'état* and were expecting another. This would mean everything in the city would stop while the opposing factions fought for control of the government. Nerves were more than a little jittery!

* * *

Vientiane has a first-row seat every time the beautiful lunar eclipse occurs. The faint yellow ring around the moon glows brightly as the earth passes between the sun and the moon.

A member of one of the Eastern Communist nations was returning to his embassy after attending a dinner party on the outskirts of Vientiane. A few blocks from his home, the quiet moonlit tropical evening was suddenly punctured with burst of machine-gun fire. Carbines and M-1's joined in the fracas.

The diplomat knew immediately that the intelligence men in his embassy had been right! The *coup d'état* WAS imminent; in fact, this was it! Swerving to the shoulder of the road, he leaped from his car, slushed through two feet of mud and water in the *klong,* and scurried across the rice paddy to a narrow lane which ran behind his home.

Crawling slowly and carefully, he made his tedious way toward the residence. Firing was increasing steadily throughout the city. As he cautiously sneaked up to the back wall of his yard, he just knew that his home, an official diplomatic residence, would be surrounded with enemy troops. As he got closer, he saw in the feeble glow of the eclipse that there were at least a dozen of the enemy in the garden. He crept closer. Boom! Boom! He flopped down on his belly and hugged the earth as tightly as he could. As he eased into the garden of his home, the diplomat stopped short, facing the "enemy" — his wife, son, and several small children of the legation's families. Shamefaced, he endured the questioning stares of the small group of women and children.

As shots continued to ring out throughout the city, the embarrassed diplomat glanced at the moon. What he thought was a *coup d'état* was a quaint local custom. The Lao believe that an eclipse is caused by a mythical frog who every few years or so, tries to "eat" the moon. To prevent this disaster, everyone grabs rifles and firecrackers and fires noisily into the sky to scare off the frog!

His light tan suit caked with mud and ripped in several places, the humiliated diplomat strode, with as much dignity as he could muster, past the wordless stares of his family and staff into his embassy.

CHAPTER TWENTY-FOUR

Facing the Firing Squad

THE LONG-AWAITED *coup d'état* finally hit Vientiane one Sunday night in February, 1965. From my quarters in the Bishop's residence on the outskirts of the city, I viewed the long line of trucks, armored personnel carriers, and tanks as they rolled into town from the Chinaimo army camp down the road.

General Khouprasith, Commandant of the Fifth Military Region, was resisting the efforts of Generals Phoumi and Siho to overthrow the Souvanna Phouma government and install their own military regime. This was my fifth *coup d'état,* and I recall it with some of the same embarrassment my Communist diplomat friend had for the lunar eclipse!

Fighting broke out Sunday night, both sides tearing loose with everything they had. Bedding down in the concrete corridors of the Bishop's house, we spent three sleepless nights listening to the 105's as they zipped over our house en route to rebel positions in the city. Answering shells and mortars landed across and down the road.

On Wednesday morning both sides stopped shooting and started negotiating. When I answered the phone, I heard the voice of Père Jean Hanique, the Oblate provincial. "Matt, if you want to get your CRS truck out of the city, you'd better do it today." When the fighting had broken out four days earlier, I had been forced to abandon the truck in the city, leaving it at Notre Dame.

"Some of the dissident soldiers are scooping up a few souvenirs," Père Hanique informed me. "Bicycles, trucks, and jeeps are being seized, and I don't think they'd be too scrupulous about taking your truck." With his assurance that life in the city was relatively calm, I headed for Notre Dame, taking with me Gerry Hickey, the CRS program assistant, and two Lao boys, Chop and Sieng. Driving Gerry's white Anglia, we headed for Notre Dame.

The streets were quiet. Except for the Khouprasith troops stationed at every intersection, and the tanks parked in front of the National Assembly, the *coup* seemed to be over. When we arrived at Notre Dame, Sieng and I climbed aboard the CRS truck.

"Let's check over at USAID for late news," I called to Gerry. As I pulled out of the driveway at Notre Dame, Gerry and Chop tagged close behind in the Anglia. I crossed Lang Xang Avenue, steered the big GMC truck around the Victory monument, and headed through the gates into the USAID compound. Spotting Charlie Dunham, chief of the Power Section and a close friend, I pulled up. Gerry slowed the Anglia and parked directly behind us, keeping the motor idling.

"What's the latest news, Charlie?"

"All's quiet, Father. They're negotiating." Charlie was red-eyed and worn out. The majority of the USAID staff had been sleeping in the compound buildings and had existed on coffee and sandwiches. Encircled by dissident soldiers fighting in the streets around the compound, the men had been unable to leave for three nights.

"I think the worst is over now," Charlie was saying. "They tell me...." Before he could finish his sentence, several 80mm. mortars landed in the street just alongside the USAID fence. Lao coolies, American staff personnel, Filipino mechanics and Thai chauffeurs tore across the compound, running in every direction. Grabbing the shirt sleeve of a Lao coolie racing in front of us, I spun him around, yelling, "Where are they fighting?"

"Yu kai, kai!"

I broke into a run and headed for the CRS truck, leaving Charlie, who spoke no Lao, standing in the middle of the USAID parking lot, yelling: "What'd he say? What'd he say?"

"Stick right behind us," I called to Gerry. Hopping aboard the truck, I set it in low gear and tore out of the compound, back into Lang Xang Avenue. When I reached the Victory monument, I glanced up the broad avenue. Road blocks were being erected. Tanks were rolling into position. Firing was increasing steadily. Circling parallel to Notre Dame, I turned the truck onto Phone Xay Avenue, thinking that we could get out of town on that street. As I neared the marketplace, I glimpsed soldiers setting up their mortars in the *klong* beside the street. "There's only one way out of town," I thought. "Dong Palan!"

The CRS truck had arrived in Laos with only its chassis and motor. My Vietnamese carpenter, a dedicated but not too skillful designer, had added a wooden bed. Unfortunately he had built the sides so high that navigation was difficult. The loss of the rear-view mirror to a light-fingered burglar had left the driver absolutely no view of rear traffic. Thus the driver was totally dependent on his navigator, who had to hang out the window, peering around the truck bed to spot obstacles in the back.

Making a quick left turn, I headed into Dong Palan Street. *"Ooery, u sci?* (Where is 'big sister'?)" I asked Sieng of Gerry's whereabouts.

"Pai talad (Went toward market)," he quickly answered.

As I slammed on the brakes, I wondered briefly why Gerry had not stayed right behind us. Realizing that my turn into Dong Palan Street had been unexpected, I thought that she might have missed seeing us and continued on to the market. Fighting had centered in Phong Xay Avenue and was concentrated in the four blocks surrounding the marketplace. If the Anglia headed in that direction, as Sieng said it had, I knew that its occupants would get hit for sure!

Hearing *"Pai talad,"* I slammed on the brakes and threw the lumbering seven-ton truck into reverse. Crash!!! The sound of twisted metal and broken glass told me, without asking, that Sieng had not looked. My navigator had answered my question stupidly, speaking the first words that came into his mind.

Crawling out of the truck, bending over to miss the stray bullets which might be flying around, I spied a very pale Gerry, and an equally pale Chop, standing beside the Anglia.

"What are you doing?" Gerry asked.

"Sieng told me you were headed for the market."

"No, we were right behind. I couldn't figure out why you stopped. The next thing we knew, the bed of the truck was coming over the hood of the car."

The Anglia, radiator leaking, headlights and hood smashed flat, and jagged pieces of glass hanging in the windshield frame, was a wreck! Since it was necessary to abandon the car, Gerry and Chop climbed aboard the truck and we continued down Dong Palan Street.

Turning into Leeville, the American housing community, I again slammed on the brakes. Stretched across the road, their rifles hoisted on their shoulders in firing position, was a platoon of soldiers. Their yellow scarves identified them as troops of the rebel General Siho of the Lao army.

I hung my head out the window, calling to them in Lao. I breathed a prayer that their eyes were good, that they would recognize us as Americans, and thus "friendlies." Stepping slowly and carefully down from the cab, I kept my hands in full sight, casually held high. With slow, measured steps, I walked toward the firing squad!

"Hao pen Khoun Pha America!" I spoke, distinctly enunciating the words, identifying myself as an American priest.

The platoon leader spat out a few words in reply, ordering me to turn around and go back where I came from. Explaining that we were cut off by the fighting behind us, and that we were headed for home just a mile down the road, I talked like a "dutch uncle" for permission to pass through the sergeant's front lines.

After several nervous minutes, the leader agreed. The sergeant shouted a terse order to his squad. They lowered their rifles and stood aside as our truck slowly moved through.

Two days later, the *coup d'état* ended. We were left with a case of shattered nerves, one wrecked Anglia, and a firm resolve to buy a rear-view mirror.

CHAPTER TWENTY-FIVE

The Pregnant Naga

THE NAGA DRAGON of mythology serves as the basis for countless Lao fables, songs and poems. Immortalized in culture and art, he is a familiar sight on Buddhist temples and in Oriental art. According to Buddhist writings, the heaven of the god Indra is on the top of Mount Meri. Below is the realm of animals and fish. At the bottom of the ocean is the palace of the Nagas, serpents who can assume human form.

Nagas have an important role in the life of the Lao. They are especially linked to rain-making. This is based on the *Megha-Sutra,* a Buddhist belief according to which Buddha gives to the Naga the power of rain-making.

Returning to Vientiane one day in 1966 after a shopping foray through the hardware stores of Bangkok, I crossed the Mekong River at Nongkhai in a tiny, flat-bottomed pirogue. As the swift current swept us a mile downstream, I mentally noted the high water level. Since my departure a few days earlier, the river had risen about six feet, and its banks were far beyond their normal level. Recalling what my Lao coolies had told me about the Naga egg, I wondered if they perhaps weren't too far wrong.

As the story went, and as it exists yet today, still unconfirmed, a Naga gave birth somewhere in the province of Vang Vieng. Returning from a reconnaissance patrol, a platoon of Lao soldiers had stumbled across an enormous white egg. No animal or being of any kind could produce an egg of this gigantic size. It had to be the egg of a pregnant Naga!

Passed from mouth to mouth, the story eventually reached my Lao construction crew. Excitedly the Lao coolies told me that the egg had been stolen. No one could find it! This was akin to sacrilege, for the Naga holds a revered position in Lao culture. Who would have the nerve to steal the Naga's egg? No one could say for sure, but of one thing my boys were certain: the Naga was angry and disaster would befall Laos!

Radio Vientiane issued reports each day on the rising waters of the Mekong. My Lao crew bought extra stores of rice and salt, and put their pirogues in running order. Vientiane would be flooded! The Naga was angry. Despite my explanations and translations of the official government bulletins which assured the populace that there was no need to be concerned, the coolies quietly said *"Doy* (Yes)" and continued to calk their boats and store their rice. The Naga was angry!

As the days passed, I began to think that maybe the Naga WAS sore! Houei Sai and Luang Prabang were swimming in six feet of water — and Vientiane had begun to build a sandbag levee. During the first week of September, 1966, the Mekong broke through the flimsy levee and poured into the Mekong Valley. Vientiane was inundated under eight feet of water. The Naga had her revenge!

Vientiane became a sea of submerged houses, floating trees, and utility poles, their lines swaying in the current of the flood waters. Only three islands existed in the city: the That Luang monument in the center of town; the

Évêché, where Bishop Loosdregt lived; and the yet unfinished new orphanage, Our Lady of Hope.

When Father Jerry Orsino, O. M. I., arrived in the soggy capital, he made what will undoubtedly go down in history as the most unusual entrance of any young cleric to mission life. Newly ordained, fresh from the States, Jerry thumbed his way into Vientiane aboard a "taxi-boat." Arrived at the provincial house, he rang the bell. Père Kolbach opened the door, and gaped wordlessly. There stood Jerry, dressed in swimming trunks, a soggy T-shirt, and a broad grin. In answer to the unspoken and bewildered look on Père Kolbach's face, Jerry calmly said: "I'm Father Orsino. I think you were expecting me." Dripping puddles of water throughout the rectory, Jerry reported for duty — damp, but dauntless!

For four weeks we shuttled around town in pirogues and helicopters. Gradually the flood waters receded, and life returned to normal. When I checked on my unfinished orphanage, I groaned at the sight of the damage which had occurred. The fifteen-acre tract itself had miraculously escaped the rising Mekong waters. It sat as a majestic island, totally surrounded by flooded fields. Taking refuge in the building, some four hundred men, women, and children, plus countless water buffalos, cattle, pigs, and chickens, had set up housekeeping. Cooking fires had blackened the freshly painted walls. Nails had been driven into doorframes for hanging wash lines. The newly planted mango and banana trees had been chewed to the ground by the cattle. In short, my new building was a wreck! As I viewed the rubble, the broken windowpanes, the soot-scarred walls, I found myself wishing that the flood had poured into the building.

Life had become quite comfortable in the "Menger Hotel." So comfortable, in fact, that the refugees refused to leave. Using one flimsy excuse after another, they hung on, indefinitely postponing their day of departure. Finally, the day the water buffalos decided to chase each other through the corridor of the new building, I put my foot down. When I threatened to call the *tomruat* (police) and put them all in jail, the refugees heeded my pleas and returned to their homes.

We set to work repairing the damage. Shoveling out the bushels of filth and garbage, we scraped the walls and floors and broke out the paint buckets. Gritting my teeth, I kept reminding myself to be charitable to these good people! After the Naga madonna and her idea of revenge, I thought there could be little more that could happen to postpone the opening of Our Lady of Hope Orphanage.

The dedication of the new building was rescheduled as we repaired the fire-blackened walls of the orphanage. Work moved ahead in usual Lao fashion (full crew one day, half crew the next, no one at all the third day), and the building gradually began to resume its pre-flood look. Nevertheless, I was in no mood for General Ma, Commander of the Lao Air Force, and his own personal ambitions to take over the Lao government.

On October 21 the sun shone brightly and the marketplace buzzed with activity. So, too, did the heavens! Dipping their silver wings, a formation of six T-28 planes flew low over the market and headed for Chinaimo army camp, five hundred yards down the road from the orphanage. As the planes passed over Our Lady of Hope, I glanced up, casually wondering why they were buzzing so low. Before I could pursue the thought, I saw the rockets tear loose from the undercarriage of the fighters. As I followed the trails of smoke, I saw them hit the army camp.

Pulling out of a dive, the planes separated and headed across town for their second target, Phong Kaeng, army staff headquarters. The planes buzzed low over the American dispensary and cut loose with rockets and machine guns, strafing and killing the unsuspecting soldiers in the camp.

Led by General Ma, the six planes caught Vientiane off-guard. Hoping that their attack would trigger a *coup d'état,* and expecting their fete of "bravery" to entice other military divisions to join them, Ma flitted through the skies of Vientiane in his little red Wren, directing his squadron in its attack.

As smoke poured forth from the Chinaimo garrison, the planes returned for a second pass. When they cut loose with their rockets, the concussion shook the entire sector of the city. Chop, my Lao coolie, and I had taken cover in the concrete halls of the orphanage building. As the concussion rocked the building, glass began to shatter and smash. Broken panes flew in every direction. We raced down the corridor and out the back door, running hard until we reached the relative safety of the thick brush.

Their work of destruction completed, the silver planes banked in the brilliant sunlight and headed back to their base in Savannakhet. Chop and I returned to the orphanage and added up the score: 110 broken windows! Thank God that the dedication had been postponed. Seeing the slivers and hunks of glass littered throughout the rooms of the orphanage, I thanked God, too, that those rooms had not been filled with toddlers and the cribs of newborn infants.

We grabbed the brooms and began once again to sweep up the debris. "Dear God," I prayed, "give me patience with these pagans."

CHAPTER TWENTY-SIX

Monsieur X

THE CLOSING DAYS of 1966 were filled with much activity and great happiness. Our Lady of Hope Orphanage, freshly painted, stood gleaming amid its fifteen acres, awaiting the arrival of the Sisters and children. All stood ready! Nurseries, dormitories, chapel, dining room, playroom, had been scrubbed, painted, and shined in expectation. The only thing now lacking was the happy sound of children's laughter. And that was on the way.

Shuttling back and forth with numerous loads of beds, mattresses, cooking pots, and babies, the Sisters happily immersed themselves and the children in their new life. Our Lady of Hope became a home.

Then came another visit from the Bishop. "Don't disband your construction crew. I've another job for you."

By "another job" the Bishop meant another large parish center. The advent of Vatican Council II had brought about changes in the liturgy. With the Mass now in the vernacular, it was necessary to have a parish for the several thousand English-speaking members of the Vientiane community. The new center would be named "Immaculata." I was to be the pastor. And this in addition to directing Our Lady of Hope Orphanage and Catholic Relief Services in Vientiane.

My Vietnamese carpenters, Chinese masons, and Lao coolies picked up their hammers, shovels, and wheelbarrows and headed for the Thadeua Road to begin construction of Immaculata Church. It was to be a large parish plant. The church would seat 350 people. Adjacent to it would be my rectory and the offices of our Catholic Relief Services program.

The political and military situation stabilized, and work proceeded according to schedule. For the moment at least, apparently Laos had got floods and *coups d'état* out of its system. Life was serene and peaceful. That is, until the police came looking for the Bishop.

Laos is deprived of many things; one of them is Brink's. How do the merchants and stores transport large sums of money? First of all, not many stores have very great sums of money to transport. And for those that do — well, let's take the Banque de l'Indochine, the largest of the five banks in Vientiane.

Twice a week all the hard currency, American dollars, that is, would be stuffed into several nondescript suitcases, then placed in an ordinary Citroën and nonchalantly driven to Wattay airport, where the money would be packed aboard a Royal Air Laos flight for Hong Kong. This system worked well, until. . . .

One morning I had difficulty getting my jeep started. I knew that the ignition points were worn and the carburetor was clogged. Finally, after much pushing by Chop and Tien, the jeep sputtered and I took off. When I stopped at a small French garage, the proprietor — and chief mechanic — greeted me with a chippy: *"Bonjour, mon père!* What is wrong with your jeep today?"

I explained to — let's just call him Monsieur X — that a tuneup was all it required, but that I couldn't leave the jeep then. I had several appointments in town that morning. We agreed that I would stop by at 11:45 a. m. He would drive me back to my CRS office and then work on the car in his garage in the early afternoon. We shook hands and I drove off.

Heading down Sam Sen Thai Street, I couldn't help thinking how different Monsieur X was that morning. He'd had a clean shave and even had used after-shave lotion! His hands were clean, rid of their customary oil and grease stains which usually ran up to his elbows. Above all, he had on a shirt! Long-sleeved, light gray in color — "just like the ones the Air America pilots wear; and the pants were the same, too!" I mused.

At eleven forty-five sharp, I pulled into the garage. "Ah, I'm sorry," said one of the young helpers. "Monsieur said that he had an important appointment in town. He could not wait for you." There was nothing I could do but drive the sputtering jeep back home. But I was sore, very sore. "Why doesn't he keep his word?" I thought to myself.

Later that day I stopped by the American Embassy. "Mac" McGuire, the Embassy security officer, hailed me.

"What do you think about the robbery?"

"What robbery?" I asked.

"Didn't you hear? They hit the Bank of Indochina."

Stunned, I listened carefully as Mac continued: "Four men in a new gray Land Rover snatched the two suitcases of money the bank was sending on the Hong Kong flight. No one was hurt, not a shot fired. They threw pepper into the eyes of the four men in the sedan who were carrying the money. That supposedly blinded them."

Chuckling to himself, Mac, a veteran security man, said: "One of the bank employees was wearing sunglasses. I wonder how pepper could have gotten into HIS eyes? And not one of the bank employees recognized a single one of the robbers!"

"Were the robbers Lao, Mac?"

"No, they were most probably Westerners. The driver was wearing a uniform, just like the ones Air America pilots wear. The police have no clues other than that. Quite a haul, Padre! Those two bags contained over half a million American dollars and negotiable checks!"

The next morning, early, I returned to the garage to leave my jeep, and to give Monsieur X a piece of my mind. Both missions accomplished, I asked him what he thought of the bank robbery. As he gave me a noncommittal, *"Quel dommage!"* I observed him closely. I noticed immediately that he was dressed once again in his "working uniform" — grimy pants, no shirt, and with grease and oil splotched all over his hands and forearms.

The bank robbery became the talk of Vientiane. Rumors sped swiftly through the offices, shops, and streets. I was not too surprised when one of my American parishioners, a young fellow noted for his sense of humor, hailed me and said:

"Hey, Father, do you think they'll put the Bishop in the clink?"

"What are you talking about, Bob?" I asked.

"Didn't you hear? They tagged the robbers' getaway car as a new Land Rover. Doesn't the Bishop own a Land Rover?"

Chuckling to himself, my friend walked away. I headed for the *Évêché,* the residence of Bishop Loosdregt, where I found Tu, the Vietnamese cook, excited and voluble. As she chattered in a rapid mixture of Lao and Vietnamese, she told me that the Bishop was at the police station!

* * *

As the national anthem drifted on, I spun the radio dial to clear the static. The Vientiane evening news dealt with the latest Communist attack, various world affairs, the activities of King Sri Savang Vatthana, and finally, what I had been waiting for.

"Today seven accomplices of the Banque de l'Indochine robbery were arrested in Vientiane. All were former French legionnaires. . . . " The broadcaster then gave the names of the seven robbers. I recognized all of the names, especially the last, for it was Monsieur X! Dressed in an Air America uniform, he had piloted the robbers' getaway car. The Land Rover he had selected for Vientiane's first bank robbery was one that a client had left in his garage a few days previously. The client was none other than Bishop Étienne Loosdregt!

CHAPTER TWENTY-SEVEN

Cotton Strings and Multiple Souls

THE THIRD COMMANDMENT is undoubtedly the easiest to obey and the most enjoyable. Sunday afternoons had long been my favorite time of the week. Church services concluded, desk work postponed until the following morning, I always looked forward to a leisurely Sunday afternoon.

On this particular day, I had climbed into my jeep for a slow drive to the village of Hat Dok Keo, eight miles from the city. For some time, Sieng had been asking me to visit his home to see his new baby. The day was sunny, with a balmy breeze blowing. I looked forward to the afternoon.

Coming to the fork in the road at Chinaimo, I turned right and steered the jeep onto the River Road, the Mekong on my right. The sound of children swimming and frolicking in the water drifted up the shore. Checkered rice paddies stretched out as far as the eye could see. The valley of the Mekong shimmered that afternoon in the soft sunlight of a late-summer day.

Sieng and his wife, Khamphet, were old friends of mine. I had known them for three years. Hardworking and poor, they were a typical family in Laos.

The jeep contentedly bounced along the chuckhole road. As I mused on my first meeting with Sieng, I recalled that it had been almost three years before. He had been working as a coolie in my construction crew when I was building the *Évêché*. Although he was honest and hard-working, Sieng was illiterate and unskilled. Thus he eked out his living by working a small plot of land and securing odd jobs as a coolie on construction crews. During the time he was working for me, we had become good friends, and Sieng had invited me to his wedding.

Marriage is of primary importance to the Lao. When the decision to marry has been made and both households concerned are agreeable to the possibility of such a match, a go-between is engaged to make the final arrangements. These negotiations center around the amount and kind of bride-price the groom must pay, and any inheritance either bride or groom may eventually expect to receive.

Being poor himself, Sieng didn't have much in the way of bargaining power. The girl he had selected came from an impoverished village family. Being one of many children, she had no wealth to offer, and no possibility of a future inheritance. Khamphet was a plain girl, completely lacking in social status. Therefore, Sieng was able to obtain her at a bargain price: two thousand kips (four dollars).

The word "love" is found frequently in the Lao vernacular, and is recorded in song, fable, and mythology. Yet the concept of love is not the sentimental emotion so highly prized in the Western mentality. In Laos, love is based more on a liking, a tolerance of an individual as compared with complete dislike or loathing.

A man does not love his wife for the joy he experiences when she is with him. She is not an asset — she is a necessity! Having a wife means having an orderly household, meals cooked, and many children, who, in turn, will provide added hands to till the fields and increase the family coffers.

When Sieng told me of his plans to marry, I asked whether he had at last found a girl he could love. He looked at me in amazement. Why should "love" enter into it?

For Khamphet also, marriage was a necessity. An unmarried girl is a source of speculation and concern in Asian society. The eldest unmarried girl in her family, Khamphet was expected to marry, reproduce, and become the matriarch of a household of children. Therefore she wasted little time on a search for a groom who provided a counterbalance to her own personality, who could offer her love and joy. Khamphet searched for a man who would be a good provider for her and her children. Thus she agreed to marry Sieng, hardworking, honest, kind, and not too unattractive. Her parents, greatly relieved at finally having married off their eldest daughter, provided her with her dowry: a sleeping mat, two pillows, one kettle, one cooking pot, and a supply of rice.

Sieng and Khamphet were both pagans. Their marriage was performed by the *moh phon,* one of the elders. Most village leaders have what is referred to as a *phon* book with all necessary ceremonies related to village life. Pronouncing the blessing, the *moh phon* tied strings around the wrists of Sieng and Khamphet, as did the members of their families and guests. This brief ceremony was followed by a feast known as a *baci.*

The focal point of the *baci* was the *khan,* a silver bowl in the center of the display of gifts and food. In the bowl were placed offerings and gifts for the young couple, as well as flowers and magic charms. Tradition dictates

that the *khan* used at the wedding feast is to be placed
between the bride and groom on their wedding night. It
is believed that removal of the bowl before the third night
and consummation of the marriage before that time, will
bring sickness and pain.

I watched with interest as the marriage ceremony proceeded. Discreetly keeping my eye on the *moh phon,* I
noticed that he turned and walked toward Khamphet. As
she sat on a bamboo mat, her head reverently bowed in
respect for this important elder, she stretched forth her
hands. The *moh phon* bent over and began tying cotton
strings to each of her wrists. The pagan belief concern-
ing the cotton strings signifies the binding of a person's
multiple souls. Tying endless threads of cotton to Khamphet's wrists, the *moh phon* chanted, "May you have a
house full of children!"

Sitting at the edge of the semicircle of guests, I glanced
at Khamphet. Her face was expressionless, her emotions
hidden. I wondered to myself if she realized the signi-
ficance of this pagan ceremony. As she embarked on the
first day of her married life, she had bound herself to
tradition, sorcery, and the fear of evil spirits. From that
moment on, her married life with Sieng would be centered around multiple taboos and legends.

* * *

Hat Dok Keo was straight ahead, and I slowed the
speed of the jeep. Winding through the narrow dirt path
which served as a main street of the village, I searched
for the hut of Sieng and Khamphet.

This village was one of the poorer along the Mekong.
The majority of the inhabitants were squatters. Unable

to purchase land, they usually cleared a bit of wild jungle and planted a small rice crop, barely enough to keep themselves and their children fed.

Through the centuries these people had battled nature and poverty in order to survive. Each family had to supply its own needs: bamboo containers were woven; the women used their looms to produce cotton cloth; herbs and roots supplemented their diets. The families grew their own food, made their own tools and clothing, and built their own houses and carts, scavenging the jungle for the basic supplies of bamboo and wood.

"Khoun Pha! U ni! U ni! (Father! Here!)"

Recognizing Sieng's voice, I turned and spotted him as he clambered down the ladder of his hut. He ran over to the jeep and excitedly welcomed me. When I saw his delight at my visit, I wondered to myself why I had not come sooner. Obviously the visit of a Westerner was a moment of great pride for Sieng and Khamphet, one they would relate over and over again to their neighbors.

I slipped off my shoes and entered the veranda of the small hut. Khamphet stood by, quiet and shy. Sieng led me to the bamboo mat and invited me to sit down. Khamphet would bring us tea.

As his wife prepared the hot tea, Sieng told me of the birth of his son. He was elated and excited. In gratitude he had taken some candles and rice to the wat (temple) as an offering to the gods.

Khamphet knelt down on the bamboo mat and poured the tea into small tin bowls. Glancing at the young wife, I noted her clean but shabby blouse, her worn skirt. They were a poor family. Poverty stalked their lives. This new mouth to feed would be an added burden.

Khamphet was pale and wan. She had not yet recovered completely from the birth of her child. The moment of birth for a woman in the Western world is one of incomparable joy and fulfillment. During the months of her pregnancy she has been coddled and cared for in a unique fashion. Her weight is carefully tabulated; the movements of the fetus are recorded in minute detail. Her diet and emotions are nurtured to an exaggerated extent for one primary reason: that she happily and healthily produce a well child. Not so in Laos!

Khamphet had continued her heavy chores until the hour of labor. Slushing through the mud of the rice paddy, she helped Sieng to plant their rice crop. Hauling water out of the village well, she lugged it into their home.

The ancient traditions passed on from generation to generation provided Khamphet with sound advice which supposedly guaranteed a healthy child and a safe delivery. For example, she was not to eat any sugar; if she did, the child would be born a glutton. Two bananas grown together on a stalk would, if eaten by Khamphet, supposedly have produced twins. She was careful not to step over the lead rope of a horse or water buffalo; if she did so, her child would have been strangled by the umbilical cord.

Thus Sieng's son began to grow in his mother's womb. From the moment of his conception he was bound to evil spirits and witchcraft.

"Are you feeling well?" I asked Khamphet.

"*Doy* (Yes), *Khoun Pha.*"

Sieng interjected: "The *me thao* ("grandmother") took care of her." Frequently one of the old women of a village assumes the role of midwife. Untrained, unskilled, these women offer little assistance to the mother at birth.

The little Meo girl on the right was killed shortly after this picture was taken.

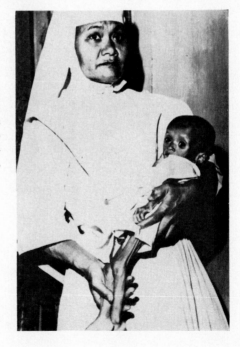

This abandoned child was one year old and weighed nine pounds when he was brought to Our Lady of Hope. Today he is healthy, strong...and loved.

But life CAN be happy!

Some of our Vietnamese orphans.

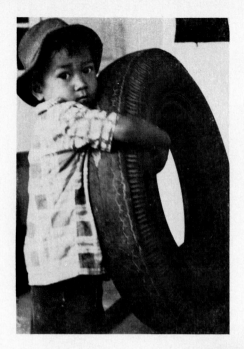

Chan La's favorite toy,
...an old rubber truck
tire.

Love thy neighbor!

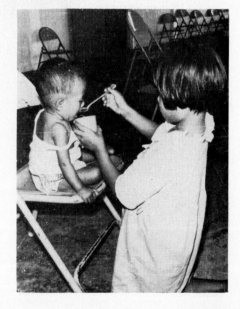

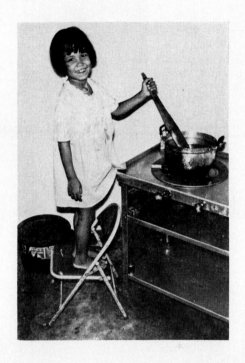

Nang Mai learning to cook at Our Lady of Hope Orphanage.

Some of the young vil-
lage girls in my train-
ing program at Dara
Som Vang.

More young girls at Our Lady of Hope Center.

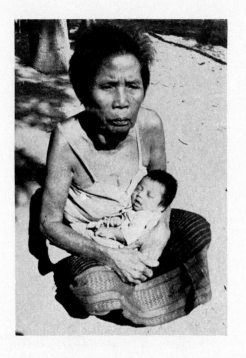

Mother and child waiting in sick-call line at Our Lady of Hope.

Leprosy!

Mother and daughter,
both lepers.

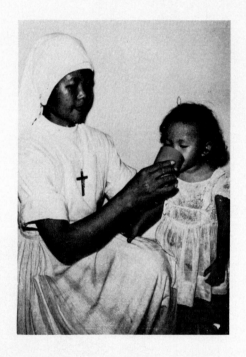

Milk always tastes better when Sister Am Mari helps one
to a drink.

The mystery of Calvary, reenacted each morning in Laos.
Through the Mass we receive the grace needed to carry
out another day in the service of the Divine Missionary.

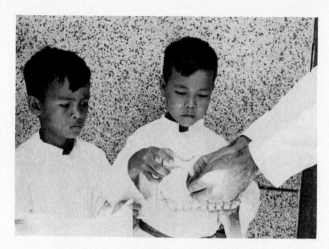

"I wash my hands in innocence...."

Getting charcoal to burn properly in a censer is a problem faced by servers all over the world.

Ling is now studying in our Oblate minor seminary in Paksane.

"The finest Bishop in the world," Étienne Loosdregt, O.M.I., Vicar Apostolic of Vientiane.

Fishing at dawn on the Mekong River.

The rivers are vital to Laos,...for drinking water, washing clothes (and bodies)....

The horror of war reflected in the eyes of a child.

Visiting one of my Laos families.

Using ancient techniques, they preside at the many births within the village.

Khamphet's village was only a few miles from a hospital in Vientiane. However, in her ignorance and blind trust in pagan beliefs, Khamphet had rejected modern medical care in favor of the traditional practices. Lying on her straw mat, she was centuries away from the consolation and help modern medicine could offer. In Lao villages antisepsis is unknown.... Evil spirits *are!*

Ordinarily the Lao woman gives birth in a squatting position, pulling on a heavy rope which is tied above her head. In some instances, a member of the family will sit on the mother's abdomen. If the child's head is slow in emerging, attempts will be made to pull the child out of the womb.

Thus Sieng's son was born. The *me thao* cut the cord with a sharp sliver of bamboo. Sieng placed the placenta in a bamboo tube and buried it at the foot of the steps.

Within hours after the child's birth, the small body was rubbed with saffron, a guarantee that the boy would have strength. A knife was placed by his head to ward off evil spirits.

Putting down my cup of tea, I asked Khamphet, "How long did you sleep by the fire?"

"One month, *Khoun Pha.*"

The practice of sleeping by the fire is the most important tradition for the mother during the period after the birth of her child. The woman is placed on a mat very close to the fire pit within the main room of the house. The fire is kept burning day and night. At no time may the woman leave the fire except to bathe and care for her personal needs. During this period she is required to bathe in hot water only, to eat fried rice and salt, and to drink large quantities of hot water. Added to the water is a root which is one of the ingredients in curry powder. It is believed that the salt and herbs, together with the hot water, keep the stomach warm and speed healing and recuperation of the mother.

Every village woman in Laos is bound to the practice of sleeping by the fire. The minimum period required for the first child is thirty days. For the second child, the period by the fire is reduced to twenty-five days. With each subsequent child, the period is decreased three to five days. It is believed that if a longer period of time were spent by the fire for the second or third child (than was spent for the first), the younger children would not have the necessary respect for their elder brothers and sisters. Thus the older children would not have the authority over the younger children which tradition demands.

The afternoon was slipping away, and I had to return to Vientiane. "May I see your son, Sieng?" I asked.

Smiling proudly, Sieng led me into the one room which served as living room, bedroom, nursery and kitchen. The infant lay in a bamboo basket, wrapped in a faded cloth which I recognized as one of Sieng's old shirts.

As I leaned over the basket, I noted the cotton strings tied to the wrists of the tiny infant. When I touched the strings, Sieng hastened to explain the good fortune they would bring his son. I straightened up, turned to the young couple, and said, "May I add the blessing of my God upon your son?" Eagerly giving their assent, Sieng and Khamphet watched reverently as I blessed this new life.

After I bade them farewell, I flicked on the ignition of the jeep and began the drive back into town. As the villages fell away and the jeep reached the outskirts of Vientiane, I reflected on Sieng's son and the hundreds of other children born today in these villages. By some miracle — or good spirit? — fifty per cent of them would manage to survive birth and embark on their lives. But tradition, habit, superstition, and evil spirits had already established the pattern that new life would take.

CHAPTER TWENTY-EIGHT

The Witch Way

ONE OF THE MOST HORRIFYING EXAMPLES of superstition and belief in evil spirits confronted me in the early months of 1967. Our Lady of Hope Orphanage in Vientiane was well established. With the children snugly and happily installed in their new home, the Sisters decided to "mobilize." Loading the rear of their truck with CRS food, clothing donated from people in the United States, plus medicines from the Catholic Medical Mission Board, the Sisters "hit the road."

Twice a week the nuns would drive southward parallel to the Mekong, visiting the villages of the delta. Setting up a sick-call line, they would treat patients with malaria, vitamin deficiencies, trachoma, stomach worms, tropical fevers. Compassionate but firm, patient yet insistent, the Sisters conveyed to the primitive mothers sound lessons in child care, hygiene, and nutrition.

One Saturday morning, I found myself heading southward toward Na Long, with Sister Marie Henri at my side. I had answered her urgent plea to accompany her to the village, listening with horror as she told me of her discovery.

With Sister leading the way, I followed along the weaving paths of Na Long to a very primitive hut, crudely built, its woven bamboo sides torn and patched, the thatched roof thin and sketchy. I recognized instantly the ex-

treme poverty of this family. We climbed the rickety
ladder, slipped out of our shoes, crossed the threshold,
and peered into the murky darkness. As my eye followed
Sister's pointed finger, I glanced toward the far corner
of the hut. There sat a young woman, her hair in wild
disarray, her thin body covered with a ragged dress and
chained to a post like a wild animal!

Instinctively I stepped back. I couldn't believe my eyes.
Who would do such a thing to another human being?
Sister motioned to me. As I followed her out the door,
we met an old-looking woman climbing the rickety ladder
up to the hut.

"This is the mother of that girl, Father," Sister Marie
Henri said.

The withered old face dipped low as the woman gave
me the traditional Lao greeting: *"Sambai, Khoun Pha."*
Motioning to the straw mat on the veranda, she invited
us to sit down.

Without waiting for my questions, Sister Marie Henri
spoke softly. "I first came to Na Long about two months
ago. There is much sickness here — malaria, cholera, fevers.
All the children have vitamin deficiencies. The people are
very poor."

Continuing, she said: "On my visit last week one of
the children teased me and asked if I was 'going to cure
the fool.' I didn't know what he meant, and so I talked
to the village elder before I left that day. He told me to
come here, and that is when I met Me Sang." She nodded
toward the mother.

Speaking gently, Sister Marie Henri said, "Me Sang's
husband died many years ago, leaving her with one child —

this girl, Leury. The mother took over the husband's chores and worked hard to keep herself and her daughter alive."

"When the girl was ten years old," Sister continued, "an epidemic of some kind hit the village. Many people were struck with fevers. As far as I can tell from what they have described, it must have been typhoid fever."

"Many people died, *Khoun Pha,*" the old woman interjected.

I turned to Sister, as she said, "Leury was one of the children struck with the fever. All of them were treated by the village witch doctor. You can imagine how useless he was. As a result, all the sick children died. That is, all except Leury."

"The *moh phi* was very angry," said the old woman. "When the people accused him of failure, he blamed Leury. He convinced the villagers that Leury was an evil spirit."

Sister broke in, explaining: "When the fever left her, Leury was not the same as before. Her mother has described her behavior to me. You know, of course, Father, that she most likely suffered some brain damage as a result of the fever. Thus she behaved like a retarded child. But the villagers are simple people. Leury's strange actions and gibberish convinced them that the witch doctor was right. Leury was an evil spirit!"

As the old woman served us warm tea in tin cups, and began to speak, I listened carefully. Her voice was soft, the words painful as she recalled: "One night Leury and I were in our house. Outside I heard many voices, shouting at us. All the people were there." Her voice trailed off.

With her hand covering the gnarled fingers of the old woman, Sister picked up the strange tale. "The villagers told Me Sang that she and Leury would have to leave.

If they stayed, Na Long would have another disaster. Me Sang begged her neighbors to let them remain. She promised that Leury would harm no one."

Her voice choked with emotion, Sister Marie Henri continued: "Finally the villagers told Me Sang they would permit her to stay on one condition. Leury must be kept in the hut and not be permitted to see or speak to anyone in the village. When Me Sang tried to protest, the elders told her that she would either have to chain her daughter inside the hut, or they would both be driven out into the forest."

"She was a poor woman, Father. She had nowhere to go, no choice. And so she chained her daughter to a post in the corner of the hut. Since that day, the girl has never been outside."

Sipping the tea, I questioned Me Sang further. As closely as I could guess, Leury was now about thirty years old. She had been chained to the post for nineteen years! Her mother tried to take good care of her, covering her with a worn blanket to protect her from the cold. If food was scarce, the poor mother would give her brain-damaged child her own portion, and go without.

For nineteen years the mother had farmed a small piece of rice paddy, scrounged in the jungle for roots and herbs, and shared her daughter's imprisonment. Because she never left the hut except to plant rice or search for food, Me Sang lived in total isolation.

Leury was hopelessly retarded. Quiet and docile, she munched contentedly on her rice, living in a world all her own, a world of fantasy that had closed the door on reality so many years before. As I observed the tired and withered face of the old woman, I knew that it was she, not Leury, who had suffered the most.

Promising that she would come each week, Sister enfolded the old woman in her arms. After saying our goodbyes and leaving behind a store of food and warm clothing, we headed back toward Vientiane.

* * *

Paganism! Witchcraft! Evil spirits! Our greatest enemies in Laos! Every pagan village has its village god, a particular spirit whom the village "rooms and boards."

The *phi* house (spirit house) is usually situated prominently in the village. Small in size, it resembles a miniature temple. It is about the size of a birdhouse and perches atop a wooden post. Every day the sacristan brings offerings of food to the god. Candles, charms, rice, eggs, bright pieces of colored papers are placed in the *phi* house to appease the potential anger of the god. It is important to keep the god contented; for if he is angry, he will roam through the village sowing sickness and death.

The burning of a spirit house is always a victorious moment in any missionary's life, but especially in the life of a young priest as he strikes the match for the first time and watches the bamboo blaze, then crumble to dead, cold ashes. It means that more pagans have rejected the cult of the gods, and now honor the one and only God!

While working in the village of Phou Kao Nang I chased the spirits out of several Meo huts. When a pagan, no matter what tribe he belongs to, asks to be instructed in the Faith, the first step is to chase out the spirits. The priest removes all objects of witchcraft from the home and burns them. Bear claws, monkey tibiae, small strips of bamboo oddly woven together, and tiger teeth were just some of the many objects of witchcraft I found in the pagan homes.

One of the most impressive moments in the chasing out of the spirits is the cutting of the "witch way." In every Meo hut there is an altar of appeasement. It is a bamboo shelf suspended four feet from the ground by bamboo strips, upon which are placed small quantities of rice, whisky, fish, water, and so on. Several strings lead from the altar up to the peak of the roof, then down to the front door. This is called the "witch way." When any of the evil witches are hungry and enter the hut, they will slide up the strings, down to the altar, and satiate their hunger there. Thus they will not be obliged to devour any of the inhabitants of the house.

The witch way probably sounds ridiculous. However, one must understand that the animistic philosophy of life attributes all sickness, death, and misfortune to irritated witches and evil spirits. Thus their altar of appeasement and the witch way take on paramount importance. To permit the priest to cut the strings and remove the altar requires a heaping dose of courage on the part of the natives. "Will the hungry witches take revenge on us? Is the priest's God powerful enough to protect us against the anger of the spirits?"

Was I shocked at the sight of Leury crouched in a corner, chained like a wild animal? Yes, of course! But not really surprised. Living in primitive villages with these people, I had often found myself confronted with their terror, their fear of the nonexistent spirits. To some of them the presence and power of the spirits was as real as the wetness of rain and the heat of the sun. Saddened, but not surprised, I could well understand how their terror of the spirits could bring such torment and suffering to a hapless mother and an innocent child.

Other children had actually died for equally foolish reasons, and equally groundless fear of and trust in the spirits. In 1956 a Meo witch doctor was "illuminated." Immediately he set forth announcing the illumination.

The "King of the Meos," he claimed, was to come in May, 1957. He would swoop up all his Meo tribesmen and escort them to paradise. The witch doctor was persuasive. He convinced the villagers that he had direct communication with the spirits. Consequently, it was useless to plow the rice fields, to store up dried fish, to gather firewood, to repair tumbling huts. The rumor spread from mountaintop to mountaintop, from village to village.

By April, 1957, the supply of rice was almost exhausted. Weeds and brush now covered the rice fields. The Meos didn't mind, for next month their king was coming!

May came — but the king didn't! July came — and still the king had not come. The tribesmen began to worry, for there was neither rice nor king.

August, September, . . . still the king did not come. The rains had passed, and it was too late to plant rice. Starvation began its costly ravages. Death was merciless. Smoke billowed as body after body was tossed on a burning pyre. All because of the king . . . who didn't come!

CHAPTER TWENTY-NINE

Two Divine Corpses

IMMACULATA PARISH CHURCH in Vientiane was nearly finished. Nestled among three acres of teak trees, the soaring peaked roof and panes of colored glass were sharply outlined in the shadows of the autumn sunlight.

After they dismantled their bamboo scaffolding, the Vietnamese carpenters set to work on the pews, while the Lao coolies tackled the mattresses. After the flood of 1966, USAID had condemned hundreds of soggy mattresses, part of the debris taken from the flooded homes of U. S. government personnel. I had spotted the stacks of soggy foam rubber in a field adjacent to the Tha Thom warehouse. The American foreman looked at me rather strangely when I asked if I could have them; nevertheless, he was relieved to get rid of his pile of fragrant Goodyear.

We spread the mattresses in the sun and waited for the rubber to dry. Cutting, piecing, using odds and ends of the foam rubber mattresses, we came up with padded kneeling pews, the first in all of Laos. My American parishioners never knew that they were kneeling on their old mattresses.

Walls painted, pews varnished, altars installed, Immaculata lacked only one thing — statues. Where could I buy

197

a Christ and a Blessed Mother? Not in Laos, certainly, nor in Thailand. Saigon?

Forty-eight hours later, I was on my way to Saigon aboard a U. S. plane. Taking off from Vientiane, we flew west to Thailand, then south, cutting back into Laos at Savannakhet. Flying two hundred miles due east over mountains and jungles (and the Ho Chi Minh Trail directly underneath), we entered South Vietnam and landed at Danang airport.

From Danang, we flew south over the Gulf of Tonkin, a mile offshore. We had an excellent view of the nearly completed Cam Ranh base. It was then that I realized why all the old Indochina hands said that Cam Ranh Bay was the finest port site in all Asia. A giant, deep cove, completely surrounded by high mountains, it afforded a narrow passage for the entry of ships. The towering mountains stopped all high winds and tidal waves caused by the frequent hurricanes and typhoons which swept through Southeast Asia.

We landed at Tan Son Nhut airport, Saigon, just before dusk. "Well, Father, we made it this far safely," said the pilot. "We'll be leaving at 0700 hours, day after tomorrow. Hope you can find your statues by then."

I arrived at the home of my good friends, Dr. and Mrs. Ky-Quan-Thanh, just in time for a delicious Vietnamese dinner. After Dr. Thanh had given me all the latest news of the family, and the war, I told him of my mission.

"Pas de problème, mon père," he quickly responded. Dinner completed, Dr. Thanh, his wife and I squeezed into his Deux Chevaux. He used his Mercedes Benz very rarely those days. It was more likely to be the target of

a grenade or plastic bomb than the poor people's Deux Chevaux.

Instead of driving directly to the statue-seller, he wanted to show me the city: the Cathedral with its imposing statue of Mary, Queen of Peace, in the park in front of it; the glittering lights of Duong Tu Do; then the waterfront with its Floating Restaurant. How the war had changed Saigon! Sure, most of the gawdy bars with the hostesses at the door were still open, but the city had lost much of the glitter and gaiety that had earned it the rightful title "Paris of the Orient." The lights seemed less bright, the gaiety forced, the number of young couples leisurely strolling down rue Catinat greatly reduced. Vietnamese gendarmes, or "White Mice," as the VC's called them, were everywhere, several at each corner. The scent of danger and the uncertainty of where the next grenade would be tossed were hanging heavily over the city.

"Mon père," exclaimed Dr. Thanh, "let me show you what the VC's have done to Cholon," the Chinese district.

Passing in front of St. Francis Xavier Church, Dr. Thanh commented: "Here is where President Diem and his brother, Nhu, heard their last Mass on the morning of November 1, 1963, just a few minutes before they were executed."

The church was locked. A couple of dim bulbs cast a feeble light against the second-floor windows of the rectory. As we reentered the car, I looked up, noticing that the neon bulb in the streetlamp was gone, shattered by bullets. The street was dark and deserted. Yet how important this spot was, and will always be, in the annals of history.

We drove slowly, winding through the narrow streets which laced Cholon together. We passed by Trung A's little tailor shop, where I had purchased a couple of sports shirts the previous year. A few blocks farther on, Dr. Thanh slowed down. "Look at Hong An's now!" I used to enjoy Hong An's, a quiet little Chinese restaurant tucked away on a side street in Cholon. With the Thanhs, I would visit Hong An's whenever I came to Saigon. The sweet and sour pork, the Peking duck, the entire Chinese cuisine of the restaurant were famous throughout Indochina. Our favorite table was next to the plate glass window in the front of the restaurant. Stretching from floor to ceiling, the window gave us a perfect view of the streets of Cholon, the hawkers peddling their wares, the pigtailed children frolicking in the street. Now that window was covered with heavy-gauge wire mesh as protection against grenades.

"Ong," interrupted Mrs. Thanh, addressing her husband at the wheel, "don't forget the statues." (". . . And the curfew, too!" I thought.)

Picking up speed, we turned back into the center of Saigon. Driving down rue Pasteur, we turned right, continued on for several blocks, then turned left down a small, narrow one-way alley. It was pitch-black. No street lights. Houses shuttered. Lamps extinguished. "A perfect place for an ambush!" I thought.

As we pulled up to a wooden-front building which served as the statue-maker's factory, with his living quarters above, we walked into a dirt-floored room. The statues looked fairly nice, and the shop had a good selection. There were several figures of Christ, statues of the Blessed Mother, St. Joseph, the Sacred Heart. The little Vietnamese tried hard to make a sale, but I could find nothing of the style or size I had wanted for Immaculata. Thanh and the little Vietnamese exchanged a couple of sentences, followed by a final bow. Dr. Thanh signaled for me to enter the car.

"There's another place, *mon père*," he said. Putting the Deux Chevaux in gear, he crept down the narrow alley, turned right, and wove down a twisting lane, narrow and dark. The alley tapered off into a footpath. After Thanh parked the car, we walked the last fifty or so steps to the second statue-maker's factory.

"Ah, here it is," exclaimed Dr. Thanh. It was a small shop, some twenty feet long by fifteen feet wide, set right on the alley. The entire front side, comprising two thick metal gates, folded open, serving as a door. At night the little proprietor would slide the two metal gates into place.

I was surprised and amazed when I entered the shop. The little Vietnamese seemed to have statues of every saint named in the litany, plus a whole corner of different-sized Buddhas and several Cao-Dai saints. We finally spotted what we wanted: a six-foot statue of the Immaculate Conception, and an equal-size body of Christ. But the statues weren't finished. They were still in the rough stage, the plaster of paris unsanded, the pinpoint holes from the molding yet to be filled in. It was then that I learned that the Vietnamese artisans do not finish their statues until they are bought. (Something like ordering a Ford with its hundreds of possible combinations!)

The owner was delighted with our interest in his statues. Then began the lengthy Oriental bargaining process — in Vietnamese, naturally. Suddenly Dr. Thanh interrupted his bargaining.

"Mon père, why don't you sit over here!" Picking up a small stool from the center of the shop, he placed it behind a tall, massive statue of St. Ignatius. "You cannot be seen here," he whispered. "This is a very bad neighborhood. If they saw an American. . . . "

He didn't have to continue. I quickly stepped behind St. Ignatius and sat, very quietly, hunching my six-foot frame together as compactly as I could. For the next thirty minutes I waited, expecting any second a hand grenade to be tossed at innocent St. Ignatius and scared Matt Menger! I listened to the Thanhs arguing volubly about price. All the while I was begging the great Founder of the Jesuits to protect his statue and the helpless little Oblate behind him.

I kept glancing at my watch: 11:10 p. m., 11:20, . . . 11:30. Curfew was at midnight, and we had a good half-hour driving back to 199 Phan-Than-Gianh street. The rapid tonal exchange between Dr. Thanh and the statue-maker stopped abruptly. Cautiously I peeked out from behind the great St. Ignatius. Dr. Thanh gave me the "all-clear" signal.

Back in our Deux Chevaux, Mrs. Thanh told me that the little man had told them to come back in a week. He just couldn't have the two statues ready in less time. They argued. He cut his time down to six days, then five. Finally the little man agreed to hire extra help. He and four other sculptors would begin work immediately. The two statues would be ready the following evening at 7:00 p. m.

Back in the Thanh residence, I had difficulty going to sleep. While listening to the 105's and 120mm.'s and the roar of low-flying jets off in the distance (and hoping they would stay OFF in the distance!), the thought struck me:

"How will I get these statues into the U. S. Air Base at Saigon (from which they would be transported back to Laos)? Only American government vehicles are allowed!"

Chewing on this latest problem all night, I rose before dawn and headed for the Cathedral to say an early Mass. Borrowing Dr. Thanh's Deux Chevaux (and his elderly maid Tu as a guide), I drove out to Tan Son Nhut after Mass. I parked the car outside the checkpoint gate, telling Tu to sit tight and scream if anyone came near the car. Dr. Thanh had warned me not to leave the car unprotected lest a passerby deposit a parcel of plastic under the hood.

Flashing my ID card at the burly AP (Air Police) at the gate, I followed the jerk of his head, which answered my request for directions. "Now that I'm in, how can I commandeer a pickup?" I wondered as I strolled down the main street of the base. There were pickups everywhere — some were parked, some drove by, steadily maintaining the base's twenty-five miles per hour military speed limit.

"Ah, the chaplain!" I thought. I stopped a staff sergeant who was passing by and asked for directions. Obligingly he offered to walk me over to the base chapel. We walked five blocks, then ten blocks, and still kept turning corners and walking some more. I was hopelessly lost. It was then that I began to realize how vast Tan Son Nhut really was.

Finally reaching the chaplains' office, I asked the corporal at the information desk if I could see the Catholic chaplain. His head bent over his typewriter, he briskly replied: "Sorry, sir. He is at a meeting."

"How about the Protestant chaplain then?"

Clack-clack went the keys. A negative shake of the head. "He's out."

"O. K. corporal. What about the Jewish chaplain?"

That question did it. The young little draftee popped open his eyes and I'm sure wanted to ask what kind of ecumenical crackpot I was. Instead, his military decorum persevered, and he merely answered tartly, "Sorry, sir, ain't got any Jewish chaplain."

"Well, I'll just wait for the Catholic chaplain!"

I picked up the afternoon's issue of *Stars and Stripes,* and time ticked by. I finished scanning the paper. Still the chaplain's door hadn't opened. I started again at page one and began reading the articles I had skipped, all the while thinking of my Deux Chevaux and the terrified little Vietnamese maid. What would she do if a VC tossed a grenade in the window? And what would *I* do?

Pulling out my wallet, I jotted down a few lines to the chaplain on one of my calling cards. "Father," I wrote, "may I see you for just a minute? URGENT!"

It took a little persuasion, but since the corporal still wasn't too sure who I was, he decided to carry out my suggestion. Picking up my card, straightening his tie, he disappeared into the chaplain's office.

Seconds later, the door flew open. Out burst a dark-complexioned, sharp-looking young chaplain, two silver bars on his collar.

"Mattia! Mattia!" he exclaimed, slapping me on the back and giving me a warm *abbracciamento a l'Italiano.*

"Mattia!" With a big smile he asked, "What are YOU doing here?"

I was so surprised at seeing HIM, that I blurted out, *"Alessandro, e tu?"* Reverting to Italian, we slapped each other on the back, both of us talking at once.

This good-looking young chaplain was none other than Father Alessandro Di Taddeo, O. M. I., a former classmate of mine in the seminary in Italy. After ordination Alessandro had been assigned to the Texas province of the Oblates. A few years later, he entered the U. S. Air Force chaplains' corps and now was Catholic chaplain at Tan Son Nhut.

Immediately he pulled together two chairs, right next to the corporal's desk. We began reminiscing about our days in Italy and Texas, and all that had happened in the nine years since we had last seen each other. He told me with great enthusiasm about his life at the many bases to which he had been assigned, and especially his front-line experiences in Vietnam.

Time passed quickly. The corporal grew weary of looking at his watch. Finally he politely interrupted, "Chaplain, your meeting?"

"Fa niente! This is more important!"

The young blond corporal, with the "Jackson" sown on his uniform, was more baffled than ever. First this lanky stranger comes sauntering in, apparently content to see any chaplain. Then he interrupts an important meeting of the Catholic chaplain. Next the two start jabbering away in a completely foreign lingo! Shaking his head, the baffled corporal pulled his typewriter forward. Clack-clack went the keys.

At nineteen hundred hours, right on the dot, a shiny new U. S. Air Force Ford pickup pulled up at 199 Phan-Than-Gian. Dr. and Mrs. Thanh and I got back into our Deux Chevaux and, with the Air Force pickup following, returned to our Vietnamese statue-maker.

He had promised to have the statues ready by 7:00 p. m. The statue-maker was embarrassed, very embarrassed. The statues were not ready. In rapid Vietnamese Dr. Thanh gave him an elaborate lecture on the importance of keeping one's word. Muttering a feeble apology, the sculptor shouted instructions to his men to hurry up! Once again, I took my seat behind the mighty St. Ignatius, and waited.

Finally the statues were finished. Then began the crating. Two young Vietnamese helpers quickly measured the exact length of the statues. Scooping up slats, they began nailing them together into huge orange-crate-like boxes. Meanwhile, Mrs. Thanh discreetly slipped over to the corner of the shop and began feeling through the deep container of excelsior. As she told me later: "You can never be sure in Saigon these days. I certainly would not want your crates to explode in mid-air tomorrow!"

With the Vietnamese statue-maker paid with a thick pile of piasters, the crates were loaded aboard the pickup and I climbed into the cab. The Vietnamese driver turned on the ignition and we were off, headed for Tan Son Nhut.

You can't beat an American pickup. With its powerful motor and roomy front seat, it was far more comfortable than the tiny, wheezing Deux Chevaux. But driving through the narrow, dark alleys of this VC-infested section of Saigon at ten miles per hour, I would have much preferred the anonymity of the Deux Chevaux. Here I was bounding along through the entire city of Saigon with those big white letters standing out in their dark blue background: "U. S. Air Force."

I was very relieved when we pulled up to the Tan Son Nhut checkpoint, ablaze with its powerful floodlights, and abuzz with its many Air Police guards. I quickly counted six rifles pointed at our pickup from all sides, front, center, rear.

"What ya got in them coffins, Buddy?" the huge corporal asked me. "More K-I-A?"

Because I was a little startled by the expression, it took me a couple of seconds to realize that "K-I-A" meant "Killed in Action." Before I could reply, the sergeant poked his hand between the slates in the "coffins" and began feeling the well-wrapped "bodies."

"I'll be damned!" exclaimed the burly corporal. "Rigor mortis sure sets in fast in this country! Move on, Buddy."

Before I could enlighten the poor AP, my chauffeur had shifted into first and we were driving down Main Street, over to Base Ops. I couldn't help wondering how my two passengers in the coffins were taking this up in heaven. I'm sure that was the first time anyone ever told the Blessed Lady that she had rigor mortis!

CHAPTER THIRTY

Sister and the Savages

NINETEEN HUNDRED SIXTY-SIX
was the Year of the Flood. Nineteen hundred sixty-seven
was the Year of the Drought. As the Mekong flowed into
the South China Sea, the wells of Laos went dry,... including that of Our Lady of Hope Orphanage!

Under the sweltering sun stood the twelve of us — nine
Lao coolies, Sister Hyacinthe, myself, and an American
named Jack. All eyes were focused on the grinding, spinning rod as it bit and chewed into the hard, dry clay. We
were tired and disappointed. "Maybe the neighbors were
right. There isn't any water," I thought to myself.

Jack turned to me and said: "Father, if you know any
saints in charge of water, you'd better start praying to
them. We're down to 215 feet now, and I doubt that we'll
find any water here."

I turned away and lit my pipe, not daring to look into
the pensive face of Sister Hyacinthe. We both knew what
those words meant! Our Lady of Hope Orphanage would
be forced to close, and our plans for the Dara Som Vang
training center for village girls would literally go down
the dry drain!

Have you ever counted how many times each day you
turn on the faucet? How many times the sink is filled?
How many drinks of water, how many hands washed?

For months now, the faucets at Our Lady of Hope hadn't even been turned on. Until six months earlier, water had not been a problem. A hand-dug open well forty-five feet deep didn't produce a lot of water, but at least it was sufficient for boiling rice and bathing babies. Then came the year of the drought and a dry well! It was then that I realized how many hundreds of buckets of water were necessary to keep sixty babies scrubbed and healthy.

The Sisters and the children were good-natured about it. Hauling water in buckets out of the nearest "wet" well, two hundred yards down the hill, they uncomplainingly rationed the precious supply, and prayed.

In a country which alternates between the deluge of the monsoon and the dryness of a desert, water is the most serious problem, and the greatest need. Billions of gallons of water flow through Laos each day swept along in the currents of the Mekong. But as yet no one has managed to harness the "Mother of Life," store it, and pipe it into the cities, villages, and homes of Laos. The mighty Mekong continues on its journey, dumping this precious liquid into the South China Sea, and leaving Laos an arid clump of clay.

When the well showed signs of going dry, we rounded up the opium smokers and began to dig deeper. Gas fumes drove even those daring souls out of the pit. There was only one solution. A high-speed drilling rig capable of boring hundreds of feet was needed. If there WAS water, the rig could tap it. Gritting my teeth in determination, I headed for USAID and started begging.

Working my way up from a friend's office in the Public Works Department, to the beige-colored carpet of the director's office, I breathed a sigh of relief as Joe Mendenhall gave his permission for use of their rig.

Thus the hot May afternoon found me, the coolies, and Jack squatting in the sun. I knew that this was our only hope. And now it seemed that we would fail again.

Before I could answer Jack, the coolies let out a yell and started to run in all directions. Out it spurted: a gusher of water! Gallons and gallons of wonderful cool, wet water!!!

We had a well at last! As the yellow mud rained down on us, I breathed a fervent prayer of gratitude, and promised never again to take any of God's gifts for granted!

* * *

The new well restored life, and lit the fires under our stoked plans to branch out. The orphanage was operating smoothly. Rapidly the cribs had filled with babies — both sexes, all shapes, sizes, and colors — Lao, Thai, Vietnamese, Chinese. Twenty village children ranging in age from seven to twelve were brought in to Vientiane and boarded at Our Lady of Hope while attending the Chinaimo school. In answer to our appeal, the Raskob Foundation in the U. S. offered scholarships which afforded these children their first opportunity to attend school.

The hour had come to launch Stage Two — the Dara Som Vang Center, a specially devised program adapted to the abilities, and needs, of young village girls.

The real key to Laos lies in the villages, for it is there that the ancient traditions and customs are preserved. The developers and leaders of Laos tomorrow are the children in the villages today. If there is ever to be a social and moral revolution, a breaking away from ancient traditions and superstitions which hinder progress, then we must begin with the very hub of family life — the woman. Dara Som Vang chose to begin with the young girl, the woman of tomorrow.

To help us understand the child of Laos, we must begin with her environment, her village, family, religion. The first significant event in the life of a child is the naming ceremony, held in the household shortly after birth. Occasionally the astrologer will be consulted to select a propitious name. Children receive their names after flowers, metals, the sun, moon, or stars. For example, "Souvanna" means gold; "Ngeun" is silver; "Boua" is the lotus flower.

For the next five or more years of her early life, the Lao child is left very much to herself. The pervading "responsibility-for-self" philosophy of Lao life is reflected in the lack of guidance the young child receives. Only one serious and concentrated effort is expended in the matter of training. At the earliest possible age, the child must be instilled with a respect for authority and reverence for elders.

The child is not pushed or even encouraged to develop her talents, to learn to use her hands and legs, her ingenuity. When a child learns to walk or swim, no mark of approval is given. It is presumed that she will form the idea that the attaining of this skill is, in itself, a reward.

By the time she is three, the child has carved a niche for herself in family life. At an early age she has found her own way and learned the necessity of cooperation and compromise.

Her parents, occupied with the necessities of tilling the fields and keeping the family supplied with food and shelter, have more or less relegated the child to the care of a grandmother or elder sister. Carried on their hip, the child is dragged along during their activities with as much interest in her on their part as in a stuffed toy or a puppy dog. She is not played with, talked to, or recognized. She is simply there, because her family has deemed that is where she should be. She is not a source of amusement or joy, but merely a small body, not capable of getting around by herself, and not old enough to be left to her own devices.

No pressure is exerted on the child to encourage her to work, study, or learn. For the most part, parental permissiveness is the norm. Without being told, the child understands that she is expected to assume her share of household responsibilities at the earliest possible age. Tending the garden, hauling water, watching livestock are all within this realm, in spite of youthful age or inability to perform these tasks well. Children learn by watching, not by instruction. If they fail to observe, they learn nothing.

The family is involved in little or no activity outside the household, and everything centers around keeping the house and working the fields. Thus there is little in the way of distraction. If a child wants company, she can find it in the rice paddy, where her father, mother, or elder brothers and sisters are working. Watching them, she eventually finds herself one day plodding through the mud inserting the tiny rice shoots.

As her mind is neglected, so, too, is her body. If she becomes ill, she may be treated with local herbs and native concoctions. If the illness is chronic, a witch doctor will be called in to determine the cause of the illness and the treatment required.

Her life is shaped and formed in much the same manner as was the life of her parents and grandparents. The code of life is respect for elders and devotion to the land. The former provides merit; the latter, survival. Beyond this, there is nothing to provide the child with a happy, productive, and optimistic future.

* * *

Her china-blue eyes flashing, Sister Hyacinthe tore loose. "They are savages!" she exclaimed, referring to her young charges.

The dignified group of American ladies were horrified. A nun speaking in this fashion! Tsk! Tsk! I could mentally hear the tongues clicking in disapproval.

Early that morning I had driven a group of American ladies to Kilometer 8 for a Cook's tour of the new Dara Som Vang Center. Contributions from families in the States had helped us to begin construction on this new training center. The edges were rounded off with a substantial gift from MISEREOR, the German Bishops' fund.

We were quite proud of Dara Som Vang! It was an idea, translated into an experimental program, dedicated to serving the needs of young girls scattered throughout the villages of the Mekong valley.

"There's nothing wrong with being a village woman, *mon père*," Sister Marie Henri had summed it up. "Our job is to make them BETTER village women!"

I had to agree with her. Laos was a land of villages, and it needed its village women. Sure, we could take a good number of these girls, feed them with a solid academic education, prepare them for city life, and then after a few years, find ourselves with the villages depleted of the young wives and mothers so desperately needed. Typing, history, bookkeeping — there's much to be said for this training. But there is also much to be said for the young woman who can raise a herd of fat sows for the slaughterhouse, market prize tomatoes and corn, and produce healthy babies, spending her evenings teaching her children to read and write. Working in these villages, seeing the people wallowing in the darkness of ignorance, I had to admit that Sister Marie Henri was right. We had to begin with the villages!

By rearranging their schedule and sacrificing their few hours of rest to take on added responsibilities, the Sisters devised a special curriculum. What did the village girl need to know? Consideration had to be given to the fact that, in the beginning, all these girls would be illiterate — wild, untrained, uninhibited. Actually their early years had been spent living in the jungle. As they entered their teenage years, their bodies developed, while their minds lingered at the five-year-age level. With girls who were ignorant, indifferent, who had the wild spirit of an unbroken filly, we would really be starting with "raw material!"

The Lao language was basic, of course! To read and write was the first step toward forcing the untrained mind to think. Sewing was another necessity. There are no shops or stores in the villages. To have a new skirt, a Lao woman had to weave her cotton thread, cut and stitch the cloth herself. Cooking, yes! But instead of wild herbs and roots, there would be fresh vegetables, which the Lao young woman could learn to grow in her own garden. A healthy body made chances of survival in the village that much greater. Therefore, personal hygiene, child care, and nutrition were added to the curriculum. Animal husbandry? Every Lao woman had the responsibility of caring for the family's livestock. Why sit by helpless as one's pigs and chickens died of cholera? One could learn to raise healthy animals, have them vaccinated against cholera, and fattened with balanced diets of protein and carbohydrates.

The curriculum finally established, I examined it with the Sisters. Our course would not be an elegant training program, a finishing school for young ladies. Rather, it would round off the rough edges of a wild, uninhibited young girl, and hopefully transform her into a disciplined, productive, thinking young woman. When she returned to her village with this training, she would serve as a beacon of hope to others. It was an ambitious program. We set to work.

The first step was to select the girls. On her regular visits to the villages, Sister Marie Henri kept a sharp eye out for girls of above-average ability. It was not easy to ascertain ability, for there was no competitive spirit among the young girls. Using her feminine instinct, judging the girls by their obvious interest in others and their eagerness to assist in caring for the people, she chose twenty of the likeliest candidates. Some were Lao, others Lao Theung, a few Meos; one or two were Kha. Ranging in age from thirteen to eighteen, they formed a motley, ragged crew. They had only one thing in common: their ignorance and their primitive background!

Securing the permission of the parents was another chore, a harder one! Suspicious and uncertain, the parents were unwilling to sacrifice a pair of hands which meant added rice production and, thus, added kips for the family coffers. Sister explained, pleaded, promised, and, eventually, persuaded.

Our twenty rough diamonds were loaded into the truck and transported to Dara Som Vang. They arrived dirty and disheveled, skeptical and uncertain. Apprehensively following Sister into their new dormitory, the girls stepped across the threshold into what, we hoped, would be the doorway to a new and better life.

Entranced with the sight of beds, their first, the girls bounced and leaped from one bed to another. The springs rattled as the "young ladies" sprang from bed to bed. Standing in the doorway watching them, I shook my head.

"Sister, do you REALLY think we can do anything with these kids?"

"Don't worry, *mon père*," Sister Hyacinthe laughingly assured me. "Let them blow off a little of that energy tonight. Tomorrow morning we'll get to work!"

The new dormitory, its freshly made curtains and cheerful feminine bedspreads, rapidly took on the look of a disaster area. The outdoor john, and the shower spigots with their now abundant supply of water, were completely foreign to the girls. Heading for the bushes, lugging a bucket of water, the girls took care of their personal needs.

For the most part, the girls adjusted well. One solid advantage was their instinctive liking for and trust of the Sisters. Gentle, patient, cheerful, never allowing their taut nerves to get the best of them, slowly and persuasively the Sisters brought the girls around to the point where we could begin.

It was a painstaking process, more painful for the Sisters than for the girls, for the nuns were keenly aware of what happiness and joy life could offer these girls if they would make use of the opportunity now being offered them. Their prayers refined into a simple, heartfelt plea: "Dear Lord, help us to get THROUGH to them!"

Thus I was not surprised, the day of the American ladies' visit, when Sister described her covey of charges as "savages." Seeing the dismay on the face of her American guests, Sister hastened to explain: "You must understand the background from which these girls have come. Let me show you."

Sister took the women in tow and led them to the new classroom, where another Sister was teaching. Two sides of the room had blackboards on which were written simple problems in arithmetic and Lao words. Sitting docilely at the desks, looking like cherubic angels, the "savages" were absorbing their daily lesson in addition and subtraction.

"If you could have seen them when they arrived," Sister began. Smiling happily, a look of achievement on her face, she proudly displayed the young ladies of Dara Som Vang to the visitors.

I myself found it hard to believe. Jumping to their feet, giving the Lao greeting in unison, they stood shyly and demurely at their desks. Then, giggling with teen-age joy, they whispered to one another. It might have been any classroom in the U. S.

Sister walked over to one of the girls and spoke. "This is Nang Ly. When she arrived at Dara Som Vang, she had never in her life sat at a table or eaten with a fork. She didn't even know how to blow her nose!" Her arm around Nang Ly's shoulders, Sister gave her a quick hug. Calling good-bye to the students, she led the ladies outside, and continued speaking to them.

"Today Nang Ly is a young lady. The dress she was wearing she made herself. As she began to develop, we saw qualities of leadership in her. So we capitalized on this natural talent by giving her more and more responsibility. Today she is the leader of her group. Trustworthy, honest, she works hard, and constantly encourages the other girls to work and study hard, too. She is emerging as a real example of what can be done with these girls. It's hard to believe that she was the most violent little savage I had ever seen when she arrived here."

With a triumphant smile, Sister Hyacinthe continued: "They are only twenty girls. But it's a beginning, a good beginning."

Born in a village of poverty and want, her conception almost an accident, rarely the fulfillment of an expression of love, the Lao child has been regarded as an inevitable end product of a society which recognizes marriage as an economic necessity. Nurtured in an environment obsessed with the primary importance of survival, she has experienced little in the way of personal affection.

As a youngster she found isolation a constant companion. Her mind was left to develop on its own. When her tiny hands should have been occupied with clever instruments designed to develop dexterity, coordination, and creativity, she found herself leading a water buffalo into a rice paddy, squatting in a garden pulling weeds, or listening to the chants and incantations of sorcerers as they drove evil spirits out of her body. Intimidated by fear and the authority of elders, she grew.

Multiple births within the family pushed her ahead faster than her body could keep pace. Perhaps along the way she lost, or others denied her, opportunities which would make her today more capable, more adept, more eager, more curious. In the pressure of family needs, her needs as an individual were forgotten. Dara Som Vang had recognized those needs.

CHAPTER THIRTY-ONE

Mission over Mugia

"FATHER MENGER? This is Tom Muldoon." As I cradled the telephone, I listened to the voice of the Catholic chaplain calling from the U. S. air base at Udorn. Fifty miles south of Vientiane, the Thailand base was a complex of runways, barracks, hospitals, and motor pools. Launching its jets and reconnaissance planes, the base pursued its assignment of bombing missions and photo-recon flights over North Vietnam.

Chaplain Muldoon continued: "This Sunday evening we are having a get-together for the Holy Name Society here at the base. Could you be our principal speaker? I'll send a plane over to pick you up." I accepted Tom's invitation and agreed to be at Vientiane's Wattay airport at two-thirty on Sunday afternoon.

Checking in at the flight desk, I asked the dispatcher, "Tony, is the plane on schedule?" My question was a rhetorical one, for Air America planes are always on schedule. Tony emitted a few curse words, then apologized.

"Chaplain, the plane came a half-hour early. The pilot knew that he had one passenger to pick up." Snapping his cigarette between his teeth, he went on: "Well, he picked up a passenger O. K., and took off. Now I'm trying to find out WHO!"

The dispatcher made a couple of brief telephone calls, then turned to me: "You don't mind a C-123, do you?

It'll be here in ten minutes. I'll have one of my men drive you to the end of the runway. We'll save time if the aircraft doesn't have to taxi in, and cut the props."

Ten minutes later the huge C-123 touched down, and I climbed aboard. Thirty minutes later, I was in Udorn. A blue Air Force sedan whisked me through the sprawling air base to Chaplain Muldoon's quarters.

Udorn was a typical Thai farming village of bamboo huts when suddenly it found itself with several thousand new inhabitants. Chosen as the site for one of the United States' largest air bases in Thailand, the town quickly got into the spirit of things. Bars, restaurants, and shops pushed the rice paddies out into the boondocks as the city fathers catered to the needs, and welcomed the cash, of the American airmen.

That evening I found myself sitting at a banquet table in the Tropical Room, one of the favorite restaurants of the base personnel. Known for its good steaks and pizzas, and its well-stocked bar, it had quickly become one of the popular spots of Udorn.

Toward the end of the meal, Jesuit Muldoon stood and introduced Oblate Menger. Gazing over the 150-odd men in uniform, I told them how grateful I was to be with them. And I was! "You men represent the U. S. Air Force. You represent America," I told them. "Here in Thailand you are separated from your families and loved ones, and enduring great hardship. Each day as you man your planes, you take the risk of death to defend the right of freedom for the people of Southeast Asia!"

After the dinner we returned to the base. Later, invited by Father Tom to stop by the officers' club for a nightcap, I sat at the table watching with interest the men of Uncle Sam's air force.

On an active base such as that at Udorn, the officers' club is permeated with an atmosphere of suspense, apprehension, and gratitude that one has made it back from the day's mission. Uncertainty lingers in the air, mingled with the shreds of cigarette smoke and the smell of stale beer. Gaiety reigns supreme, and any guy who dares reveal his true feelings is "chicken."

As I sipped my beer, I watched the pilots in the haze of the dimly lit room. After ordering a round of drinks, they would shake the dice in their box, set up a yell for the "sucker" who lost the round, and then order yet another round. Some were challenging others to an "afterburner," the pilots' famous concoction: a shot of whisky, followed by a shot of brandy — flaming! The trick was to get the glass of brandy to the lips and down the gullet without setting fire to one's throat and mouth! Tinkletinkle went the dice. . . . Out came the beer.

Over at the long bar there was more laughter and singing than usual. A tall, lanky, red-faced captain from Texas, he had just completed his one hundredth, and last, mission over North Vietnam. In a few days he would be on his way home. But not before he got a good "bash."

Tradition dictates that the lucky guy who survives his hundredth mission has to treat his buddies to his own farewell party. More drunk with relief at his good fortune than with the booze, the pilot was tying one on in wild Texas style.

Slopping whisky and beer into glasses, the little Thai bartender hustled up and down the bar, double-timing it,

chattering a mile a minute in Thai as he attempted to cope
with the endless orders being fired at him. Occasionally
the guest of honor would sail through the air, grinning
happily as his buddies tossed him up and down, shouting
and singing, "For he's a jolly good felloooooo."

The guest of honor stood perched atop the bar, clutch-
ing a glass of whisky against his flight suit, his head brush-
ing the ceiling of the club. Swaying from side to side, his
eyes glazed and happy, he directed his buddies in the singing of "The Yellow Rose of Texas."

The door opened, and in walked a handsome, crew-cut,
strapping blond major. Chaplain Muldoon signaled him
over to our table and introduced him as "Ed." We shook
hands, and he sat next to me. Still in his flight suit, he
told us he had just returned from a recon flight over North
Vietnam.

"You know, Major, I certainly admire you," I said to
him. "I'd be darned scared to fly through that ack-ack and
SAM missiles. It takes a lot of courage!"

He cut me short. "Father, you see these men? There
are over a hundred here tonight, most of them still in their
flight suits. If any one of them tells you he's not scared
when he climbs into that cockpit, he's a damn liar!"

His face taut with emotion, Ed went on. "Tonight was
my forty-third mission into North Vietnam in fifty-one
days. I've been scared forty-three times! Take tonight, for
example. I had a recon mission over the Mugia Pass. With
mountains on either side, that pass is damn small. The
Viets know exactly where we have to fly, right between
those two mountain peaks. And they know what altitude
we have to maintain on a recon mission. They have nests
of AA's (anti-aircraft) on both sides of that pass and on

the flanks of each mountain. Their guns are just sitting
there waiting for us!"

Ed hailed the waiter, ordering another Scotch on the
rocks. "If I weren't sure I was in the state of grace...,
Padre, you couldn't pay me to fly across that border!"

Taking a quick gulp that half-emptied his fresh drink,
Ed continued softly: "That's why I go to Mass and Communion every morning, Father. When my instruments tell
me I'm crossing into North Vietnam, I go in with my guts
tightened and saying an act of contrition."

Nodding toward the merrymakers at the bar, he said,
"See those guys, Father?" I glanced at the boisterous group
of the hundredth mission party as I heard Ed say, "Those
guys tonight are scared stiff, because tomorrow they have
to go right back to that hell they visited today."

The farewell party was reaching its conclusion. Grabbing the guest of honor, his buddies gleefully ripped up
the seams of his flight suit. With the pants hanging in
tattered strips down his legs, his white shorts showing
through the gaps, he solemnly marched out of the officers'
club. Falling into line behind him, the guests lifted up
tattered pieces of his pants' legs. Holding them high,
marching in cadence, the group of pilots filed out of the
bar to the tune of "Here Comes the Bride."

The pilot headed for the sack, to sleep the dreamless
sleep of the lucky guy who has racked up his hundredth
mission — and is headed for home.

Back in Vientiane, I considered the situation in Laos,
about two-thirds of it today controlled and occupied by
the Communists. The Communists had never honored the
Geneva Agreements of 1954 and of 1962, which guaranteed the neutrality and independence of Laos. Only the

presence of the United States in Southeast Asia has pre-vented the complete take-over of Laos by the Communists.

At the rectory, I tackled the mail which had arrived during my absence. As I picked up one letter, I noticed the postmark "Bruneau, Idaho." Slitting the envelope, I began to read the brief note from my friends Joe and Leona Turner. Their son Ken, a pilot, had been killed in Vietnam just a few weeks before. His plane went down on a mission over North Vietnam, and was never recovered. When I had written Ken's parents, I had tried to send them some words of comfort and assure them of my prayers for their hero-son and for themselves.

"Please forgive us for being so tardy," Leona wrote. "We live on a ranch and have cattle to care for. The sum-mer is long and hot. We do our own work, and we are not as young as we once were, so it's easy to put things off. We enjoy our work, and we thank God, for it has been a great aid to us."

As I thought about the pilots in the club at Udorn, Leona's words had even more personal meaning for me. "Losing Ken is a heavy cross for us to bear," she wrote, "but he was a very good and dedicated soldier. So we, too, will be good soldiers. Ken is in heaven, and that knowledge helps us strive even harder with God's grace to merit eternal life. It is also such a comfort. Our hearts go out to people of little or no faith when they lose a loved one. What a blank space there must be! As much as we regret the loss of so many of our wonderful boys, I have a feeling that their sacrifice will not be in vain, that it will stem the tide of Communism. Sad to say, I'm afraid so many of our people do not know what Communism is and what a great evil it is. Pray God we never have to learn the hard way!"

I put Leona's letter down on my desk. Patriotism, courage, bravery — corny words these days, some say. But, thank God, those words still had meaning to the Joe and Leona Turners, to the Kens and Eds, and the men of Udorn.

Flipping open my breviary, I began the prayers of Compline, begging God that the people of America would never know first hand the evils of Communism. And praying that they would never learn the hard way!

The author can be reached at the following address:
REV. MATT J. MENGER, O. M. I.
MISSION CATHOLIQUE
VIENTIANE
LAOS